Microsof

Users

Unleash Your Inner AI Ninja, Master Microsoft Copilot and Transform the Way You Work

Patrick K. Romero

Copyright

Disclaimer

The material offered in this guidebook is intended for general informative purposes only. While the author has worked to give accurate and up-to-date information, technology is always improving, and some elements may change over time. The author makes no representations or guarantees of any kind, explicit or implied, regarding the completeness, accuracy, reliability, appropriateness, or availability with respect to the information, instructions, or accompanying images included in this guidebook for any purpose.

Any reliance you put on such material is consequently solely at your own risk. The author shall not be accountable for any mistakes, omissions, or inaccuracies in the information included within this handbook, nor for any losses, injuries, or damages originating from its presentation or use.

Microsoft Excel is a registered trademark of Microsoft Corporation. This guidebook is not related with, approved, sponsored by, or in any way formally linked with Microsoft Corporation.

Table of Contents

CHAPTER ONE

Welcome to the Copilot Revolution

Hold on tight, tech fans and people who are just interested! We're about to start an exciting adventure in the world of Copilot, Microsoft's AI helper that's not just changing the rules but writing them from scratch.

Copilot: The AI Assistant That's (Finally) Worth Talking To

Don't forget Clippy? That happy little paperclip that showed up out of nowhere in Microsoft Word and gave you advice you didn't ask for? Yes, we also try to forget about him. That being said, Clippy, bless his persistent paperclip soul, was only the first mistake Microsoft made in their attempt to make a truly helpful AI helper. Moving forward, we now have Copilot, a sleek and smart AI that is light-years better than its awkward predecessor. Copilot is like having a smart study assistant, a creative writing partner, and a coding expert all in one easy-to-use package. No more silly animations or ideas that make you feel bad. People say that Copilot is all business, but it has a personality that makes it feel more like a friend than a cold, calculated machine.

The "Clippy" Evolution:

From Comic Relief to Productivity Powerhouse

So, how did we get from Clippy's cringe-inducing pranks to Copilot's amazing capabilities? It's been a long road, paved with advances in machine learning, natural language processing, and artificial intelligence study. Copilot reflects the culmination of decades of progress. It's the result of Microsoft's relentless chase of a truly intelligent assistant that can understand our needs, predict our obstacles, and help us achieve our goals.

Real-World Impact:

Case Studies and Anecdotes

But don't just take our word for it. Copilot is already making changes in the real world, changing how people work, create, and interact.

- Marketing teams are using Copilot to discuss catchy ideas, draft social media posts, and even make full marketing campaigns.
- Software workers are depending on Copilot to write better code, fix faster, and even create full functions with a single prompt.
- Students are leveraging Copilot's research skills to gather information, summarize articles, and even draft essays (though we don't suggest depending on it for all your homework).

These are just a few examples of how Copilot is changing efficiency and creativity across businesses.

Why This Book?

A Comprehensive, Witty, and Practical Guide

Now, you might be thinking, "Why do I need a book about Copilot? Can't I just figure it out on my own?" Sure, you could. But why go it alone when you can have a knowledgable (and slightly odd) guide by your side? This book is your all-access pass to the world of Copilot. We'll cover everything you need to know, from the absolute basics to the most advanced skills, all in a way that's both useful and exciting.

Who This Book Is For:

Tech Newbies, Seasoned Pros, and Everyone In Between

Whether you're a tech newbie who's just starting to dip your toes into the AI waters or a seasoned pro who's always looking for new ways to improve your workflow, this book is for you. We'll meet you wherever you are on your tech journey and help you harness Copilot's power to achieve your goals. We promise to keep the words to a minimum and the fun running easily.

What to Expect:

A Deep Dive into Copilot's Features, Potential, and Future

In the pages that follow, we'll embark on a comprehensive exploration of Copilot's capabilities. We'll cover:

- **Installation and setup:** Getting Copilot up and running on your system.
- **Navigating the interface:** A guided tour of Copilot's features and tools.
- **Mastering prompts:** The art of crafting effective instructions to get the most out of Copilot.
- **Copilot in action:** How to use Copilot for everything from writing emails to building apps.
- **Advanced techniques:** Customization, troubleshooting, and integration with other tools.
- **The future of Copilot:** Emerging trends, ethical considerations, and the impact of AI on the workplace.

By the end of this book, you'll be a Copilot pro, ready to harness the power of AI to transform the way you work and create.

A Roadmap for the Journey:

From Installation to Advanced Tricks

Think of this book as your path to Copilot success. We'll start with the basics, building a strong basis for your AI journey. Then, we'll gradually ramp up the complexity, presenting you to advanced methods and secret features that will take your Copilot skills to the next level. But don't worry, we won't leave you stuck in the technical woods. We'll be with you every step of the way, giving clear explanations, useful tips, and a good dose of fun to keep things light and entertaining. So, are you ready to join the Copilot revolution? Let's dive in!

CHAPTER TWO

Installation and Setup:

Getting Started with Copilot (and Avoiding Tech-Induced Meltdowns)

Alright, folks, now that we've gushed over Copilot's brilliance, it's time to roll up our sleeves and get down to business. Don't worry, we won't leave you hanging with a dry, jargon-filled instructions. This chapter is your helpful guide to getting Copilot installed, set up, and ready to work its magic.

The Copilot Shopping List: What You'll Need (Besides a Sense of Adventure)

Before we dive into the installation process, let's make sure you have everything you need. Think of it as packing your digital backpack for this AI-powered expedition:

- **A Compatible Device:** Copilot is a bit picky about who it hangs out with. Make sure your computer meets the minimum system requirements (which we'll spell out in plain English, promise).
- **Compatible Software:** Copilot works well with certain software. We'll tell you which programs it gets along with best.
- **A Subscription (Maybe):** Depending on which Copilot type you choose, you might need a membership. But don't worry, we'll break down the choices and help you find the best fit for your wants and price.

Installing Copilot:

A Step-by-Step Guide (with a Side of Humor)

Now for the fun part: actually getting Copilot on your machine. Don't worry, it's not rocket science. Just follow these simple steps:

1. **Download:** Head to the official Copilot website and click the big shiny "Download" button. (Don't worry, we'll provide the exact link – no scavenger hunt required.)
2. **Install:** Run the installer and follow the on-screen instructions. It's like a Choose Your Own Adventure book, but with fewer dragons and more software agreements.
3. **Troubleshooting (Just in Case):** If anything goes wrong (and hey, it happens to the best of us), don't panic. We've got troubleshooting tips that even your grandma could understand.

Initial Setup:

Personalizing Your AI Sidekick

Congratulations, you've installed Copilot! Now it's time to make it your own. This is where the fun really begins.

- **Name That AI:** Give your Copilot a name. Will it be Alfred, your trusty butler, or J.A.R.V.I.S., your high-tech assistant? The choice is yours.

- **Voice & Personality:** Choose a voice that soothes your soul (or tickles your funny bone). Want Copilot to sound like a British butler or a wise-cracking comedian? You got it.
- **Preferences:** Tell Copilot what kind of help you need. Do you want writing suggestions, coding assistance, or a mix of both? Copilot aims to please.

First Encounters:

A "Getting to Know You" Session

Now that Copilot is all settled in, it's time for a little chit-chat. Try out some basic commands and see what this AI wonder can do.

- **"Write me an email about..."**
- **"Summarize this article for me."**
- **"Help me brainstorm ideas for..."**

Don't be shy! The more you interact with Copilot, the better it gets at understanding your needs and preferences.

Ready, Set, Copilot!

By now, you should have Copilot installed, set up, and ready to go. You've taken your first steps into the exciting world of AI-powered efficiency. So, what are you waiting for? Let's dive in and discover all the great things you can do with your new AI partner!

CHAPTER THREE

Navigating the Copilot Interface:

Your Command Center for AI-Powered Productivity

Now that you've successfully installed and set up Copilot, it's time to take a tour of its interface and discover the tools and features that will help you unleash your creative and productive potential. Think of this chapter as your roadmap to traversing the Copilot interface, understanding its various components, and mastering the art of constructing effective prompts.

The Copilot Dashboard:

Your Visual Command Center

The Copilot interface is your central hub for interacting with your AI assistant. It provides a distinct and organized layout of all the essential tools and features, making it simple to locate what you need swiftly and efficiently.

Key Elements of the Copilot Dashboard:

- **Prompt Bar:** This is where the magic happens – the text field where you enter your prompts and instructions for Copilot.
- **Command Center:** A comprehensive list of Copilot's built-in commands and their functions.

- **Customization Options:** Personalize Copilot's appearance, behavior, and integrations to match your workflow and preferences.
- **Activity Feed:** A chronological record of your interactions with Copilot, including past prompts, responses, and generated content.
- **Help & Support:** Access documentation, tutorials, and other resources to help you get the most out of Copilot.

The Prompt Bar:

Where the Magic Happens

The prompt bar is the heart of the Copilot interface, where you communicate your needs and desires to your AI sidekick. Here are some tips for crafting effective prompts:

- **Be clear and concise:** State your request or instruction in a straightforward and unambiguous manner.
- **Provide context:** The more context you give Copilot, the better it will understand your intent and generate relevant responses.
- **Use keywords:** Include relevant keywords and phrases to guide Copilot in the right direction.
- **Be specific:** The more specific you are, the more precise and accurate Copilot's response will be.

- **Use natural language:** Avoid technical jargon and complex phrasing. Speak to Copilot as you would to a human assistant.

Command Center:

A Comprehensive List of Copilot's Built-in Commands

Copilot comes with a built-in set of commands that you can use to control its behavior and access its various features. These commands are a powerful way to streamline your workflow and get the most out of your AI assistant.

Here are some of the most useful Copilot commands:

- **Write:** Generate different creative text formats, like poems, code, scripts, musical pieces, email, letters, etc.
- **Summarize:** Summarize factual topics or create summaries of articles, books, etc.
- **Translate:** Translate text from one language to another.
- **Answer:** Answer your questions in an informative way, even if they are open ended, challenging, or strange.
- **Explain:** Explain a concept or idea in a clear and concise way.
- **Brainstorm:** Generate ideas for creative projects, marketing campaigns, business strategies, etc.
- **Rewrite:** Rewrite text in a different style or tone.
- **Debug:** Help you debug your code and identify errors.
- **Fix:** Fix errors in your code automatically.

Customization Options:

Personalize Copilot to Your Preferences

Copilot offers a variety of customization options that enable you to customize its appearance, behavior, and integrations to your specific requirements and preferences. Here are some of the main customization options:

- **Voice and Personality:** Choose from a variety of voices and personalities for Copilot.
- **Theme:** Select a theme that matches your personal style.
- **Integrations:** Connect Copilot with your favorite tools and applications.
- **Keyboard Shortcuts:** Create custom keyboard shortcuts for frequently used commands.

Activity Feed: Your History with Copilot

The activity summary provides a chronological record of your interactions with Copilot. This can be a valuable resource for reviewing past prompts, responses, and generated content. You can also use the activity feed to monitor your progress and see how you've been using Copilot over time.

Help & Support: Get the Most Out of Copilot

The help and support area offers access to literature, lessons, and other tools to help you get the most out of Copilot. You can also call the Copilot support team if you have any questions or need help.

By knowing the Copilot interface and its various components, you'll be well on your way to harnessing the power of AI to improve your productivity and creativity.

CHAPTER FOUR

The Power of Prompts:

Talking to Your AI Like a Pro (and Getting It to Do Your Bidding)

Alright, folks, buckle up! We're about to dive into the secret sauce of Copilot mastery: the art of prompt engineering. Think of it as learning to speak your AI sidekick's language – the key to unlocking its full potential and getting it to do your bidding (within reason, of course). No Jedi mind tricks required, just a little finesse and a dash of creativity.

The Art of Prompt Engineering: It's Not Just What You Say, It's How You Say It

It takes more than merely putting text into a box to be prompt; prompt engineering involves creating instructions that Copilot can comprehend and follow efficiently. Imagine it like providing instructions to a really smart buddy who is a little literal-minded. You want to be precise, succinct, and free of any ambiguity that can have hilarious (or disastrous) repercussions.

But fear not, all you need to learn this ability is a basic understanding of language. You'll quickly become an expert at conversing with Copilot with a little practice and the advice we're going to provide you.

Prompt Types:

The Copilot Conversation Starter Kit

Just like human conversations, Copilot interactions can take many forms. Here are a few common prompt types to get you started:

- **Questions:** Ask Copilot for information, explanations, or suggestions. (Example: "What are the benefits of using solar energy?")
- **Commands:** Tell Copilot to perform a specific task. (Example: "Write a summary of this article.")
- **Statements:** Provide context or background information for Copilot. (Example: "I'm writing a blog post about sustainable living.")

Specificity vs. Generality: Finding the Sweet Spot

When crafting prompts, it's important to find the right balance between specificity and generality.

- **Too General:** "Write something about climate change" – This could result in a broad overview, a personal essay, or a scientific report.
- **Too Specific:** "Write a 500-word essay on the impact of rising sea levels on coastal communities in the Pacific Northwest, citing at least three peer-reviewed studies" – This might be too restrictive, limiting Copilot's creativity.

Somewhere in the center is where the sweet spot is. Give Copilot just enough guidance to get it where it needs to go while yet allowing it some flexibility and creativity.

Examples and Exercises:

Practice Makes Perfect (or at Least Pretty Darn Good)

Let's put our newfound prompt engineering skills to the test with a few real-world scenarios:

1. **Scenario:** You're writing a marketing email for a new product.
    - **Bad Prompt:** "Write a marketing email."
    - **Good Prompt:** "Write a persuasive marketing email introducing our new eco-friendly laundry detergent, highlighting its key benefits and offering a special discount for first-time buyers."
2. **Scenario:** You're debugging a piece of code.
    - **Bad Prompt:** "Fix my code."
    - **Good Prompt:** "I'm getting an error message that says 'SyntaxError: invalid syntax' on line 15. Can you help me identify and fix the problem?"
3. **Scenario:** You're brainstorming ideas for a blog post.
    - **Bad Prompt:** "Give me some blog post ideas."
    - **Good Prompt:** "I'm looking for creative blog post ideas about sustainable travel. Can you suggest some topics or angles I could explore?"

By practicing with different scenarios and experimenting with different prompt types, you'll quickly develop a knack for communicating effectively with Copilot.

The Prompting Playground: It's Time to Experiment!

After mastering the fundamentals of prompt engineering, it's time to unleash your inner artist. Feel free to experiment by trying out various prompts and seeing what works. There are many options available to you, and the more you use Copilot, the more its hidden capabilities will become apparent.

CHAPTER FIVE

Keyboard Shortcuts:

Unleashing Your Inner Copilot Ninja (No Nunchucks Required)

Alright, fellow keyboard warriors, it's time to level up your Copilot game with the ultimate weapon: keyboard shortcuts. These nifty little combos are the secret to lightning-fast navigation, effortless command execution, and impressing your colleagues with your digital dexterity. (Think of it as Copilot kung fu, but without the awkward karate chop noises.)

Why Bother with Shortcuts? Because Time is Money, Honey

Let's face it, no one has time to spend paging through text pages or clicking through many options. Your express route to Copilot productivity is a keyboard shortcut that can help you complete things faster than a hummingbird on caffeine. Furthermore, it's a fact that learning shortcuts is just simple awesome. It's similar to have insider information that distinguishes you from common people who depend on their mouse. You will be the digital domain's master and the envy of the workplace.

Copilot's Keyboard Shortcut Cheat Sheet: Your Secret Weapon

Here's the moment you've been waiting for: the master list of Copilot keyboard shortcuts. We've divided them into categories for easy reference, but feel free to jump around and discover your favorites.

Navigation Ninjutsu:

- **Toggle Copilot:** Ctrl + . (or Cmd + . on Mac) – Summon or dismiss your AI sidekick with a flick of the wrist.
- **Cycle through suggestions:** Alt +] or Alt + [– Quickly browse through Copilot's brilliant (or sometimes questionable) ideas.
- **Accept suggestion:** Tab – Embrace Copilot's wisdom and insert the suggestion into your text.
- **Reject suggestion:** Esc – Politely decline Copilot's offer and continue typing your own masterpiece.
- **(More to Come!)** We'll be adding more navigation shortcuts as Copilot evolves. Stay tuned!

Commando Combos:

- **Generate code:** Ctrl + Enter – Watch Copilot work its coding magic and conjure up snippets of code based on your instructions.

- **Explain code:** Ctrl + Shift + E – Get Copilot to break down complex code into bite-sized, easy-to-understand explanations.
- **Refactor code:** Ctrl + Shift + R – Let Copilot tidy up your code and make it more efficient and readable.
- **(More to Come!)** As Copilot's capabilities expand, so will its command shortcuts.

Customization Kung Fu:

- **Open settings:** Ctrl +, – Fine-tune Copilot's behavior and appearance to match your preferences.
- **Create custom shortcuts:** Ctrl + Shift + P then type "Copilot: Keyboard Shortcuts" – Unleash your inner power user by creating personalized shortcuts for your favorite commands.

Remember: These are just a few of the many keyboard shortcuts available in Copilot. Explore, experiment, and find the ones that work best for you. Before you know it, you'll be navigating Copilot with the speed and grace of a digital ninja.

Pro Tip: Keep this chapter handy as a reference. You can even print out the shortcut list and stick it on your monitor for quick and easy access.

Custom Commands:

Become a Copilot Maestro with Personalized Shortcuts

Alright, power users, it's time to unleash your inner Copilot maestro! While Copilot's built-in shortcuts are helpful, the true beauty comes in customizing your own customizable shortcuts for commonly performed activities. Think of it as writing your own Copilot symphony — a harmonic combination of instructions that simplify your workflow and elevate your productivity to new heights.

Why Custom Commands? Because You're Not a One-Size-Fits-All Kind of Person

Let's face it: we're all unique snowflakes with our own idiosyncrasies and preferences. What works for one Copilot user may not work for another. That's where custom commands come in. They enable you to personalize Copilot to your individual requirements, generating shortcuts that suit with your workflow and personal style. Whether you're a code-slinging developer, a data-crunching analyst, or a word-wrangling writer, custom instructions may accelerate your productivity and make Copilot seem like an extension of your own mind.

Crafting Your Custom Command Masterpieces:

A Step-by-Step Guide

Ready to unleash your inner Copilot composer? Here's how to create your own personalized shortcuts:

1. **Identify Your Power Moves:** Start by identifying the actions you perform most frequently in Copilot. Are you always summarizing articles, generating code

snippets, or brainstorming ideas? These are prime candidates for custom commands.

2. **Choose Your Words:** Give your command a clear, concise name that reflects its function. (Example: "Summarize Article" or "Generate Code Snippet")
3. **Define the Action:** Specify exactly what you want Copilot to do when you execute the command. This might involve providing a specific prompt, selecting a particular tool, or even triggering a sequence of actions.
4. **Assign a Shortcut:** Choose a keyboard shortcut that's easy to remember and doesn't conflict with any existing shortcuts.
5. **Test and Refine:** Try out your new custom command and see how it works. If it's not quite perfect, don't worry! You can easily edit and refine it until it's just right.

Examples of Custom Command Brilliance:

Need some inspiration? Here are a few examples of how you can use custom commands to supercharge your Copilot experience:

- **"Blog Post Outline":** Generate a detailed outline for a blog post based on a topic or keyword.
- **"Social Media Post":** Craft a catchy social media post with relevant hashtags and emojis.

- **"Data Analysis Report":** Analyze a dataset and generate a comprehensive report with key insights.
- **"Code Refactoring":** Automatically improve the readability and efficiency of your code.
- **"Meeting Notes":** Summarize key points and action items from a meeting transcript.

The possibilities are endless, so get creative and start crafting your own custom command masterpieces!

Pro Tip

Share your custom commands with your colleagues or the wider Copilot community. You might just inspire others and discover new ways to use Copilot that you never imagined.

Unleash Your Inner Maestro:

With custom commands, you can convert Copilot into a customized productivity powerhouse that's precisely tuned to your requirements and workflow. So, what are you waiting for? Start exploring, unleash your imagination, and become the Copilot master you were destined to be!

Voice Commands (If Applicable):

Unleash Your Inner Dictator (In a Good Way)

Okay, guys, get ready to forsake the keyboard and embrace the power of your voice! If you're fortunate enough to have a Copilot version with voice command capabilities, you're in for a treat. This hands-free way to AI engagement is not only very convenient but also unexpectedly enjoyable.

Why Talk to Your Computer

Sure, typing is fine and all, but sometimes you just want to step back, relax, and let your voice do the job. Maybe your hands are occupied wrestling a kid, or maybe you're simply bored of gazing at a screen. Whatever the cause, voice commands provide a refreshing contrast to the clickety-clack of keyboard input.

But voice commands aren't simply about convenience. They may also enhance your productivity by enabling you to multitask like a pro. Imagine typing an email while simultaneously preparing your morning coffee or discussing ideas for your next project while taking a leisurely walk.

Copilot Voice Commands: Your Verbal Toolkit

Ready to unleash your inner dictator (in a good way)? Here's a glimpse into the world of Copilot voice commands:

- **Activation Phrase:** "Hey Copilot" (or whatever your chosen wake word is) – This is how you get Copilot's attention.
- **Basic Commands:**
  - "Write an email to..."
  - "Summarize this article."
  - "Generate code for..."
  - "Brainstorm ideas for..."
- **Navigation Commands:**
  - "Scroll up/down"

    - "Go to next/previous line"
    - "Select all"
- **Editing Commands:**
    - "Delete that"
    - "Undo/redo"
    - "Replace [word/phrase] with [word/phrase]"

Pro Tips for Voice Command Virtuosos:

- **Speak Clearly:** Enunciate your words and speak at a natural pace.
- **Be Specific:** The more precise your instructions, the better Copilot will understand your intent.
- **Use Natural Language:** Don't try to sound like a robot. Speak to Copilot as you would to a human assistant.
- **Train Your Voice:** If Copilot is having trouble understanding you, spend some time training its voice recognition.
- **Have Fun:** Don't take it too seriously! Experiment with different commands and see what you can create.

The Future of Voice:

A World of Possibilities

Voice commands are still in their early stages, but their potential is enormous. As voice recognition technology continues to improve, we can expect to see even more sophisticated and intuitive voice interactions with Copilot.

Imagine a future where you can simply speak your thoughts and ideas, and Copilot will transform them into polished prose, functional code, or stunning visuals. The possibilities are truly limitless.

A Note for the Keyboard Loyalists:

If you're not quite ready to ditch your keyboard, that's perfectly fine. Copilot still offers a plethora of keyboard shortcuts and other input methods to suit your preferences. But if you're feeling adventurous, we encourage you to give voice commands a try. You could simply be shocked at how much you appreciate it.

So, whether you're a voice command enthusiast or a keyboard loyalist, Copilot has something for everyone. Let's continue our journey and explore even more ways to harness the power of AI in your daily work.

Hidden Gems:

Copilot's Secret Stash of Tricks (Shhh, Don't Tell Anyone)

Alright, fellow adventurers, get ready to dive into Copilot's treasure chest of hidden features and shortcuts. These aren't your run-of-the-mill commands; these are the secret handshakes, the whispered passwords, the backdoor entrances to Copilot's most powerful capabilities.

Why Unearth Hidden Gems? Because Ordinary is Boring

Sure, Copilot's basic functions are impressive, but who wants to settle for ordinary? By uncovering these hidden gems, you'll unlock a whole new level of productivity, creativity, and sheer awesomeness. You'll become the Copilot whisperer, the one who knows all the secret codes and hidden passageways.

Unveiling the Hidden Gems: A Treasure Map for Copilot Explorers

Get your magnifying glass ready, because we're about to embark on a treasure hunt through Copilot's interface. Here are a few of the hidden gems we've unearthed:

1. **The "I'm Feeling Lucky" Button:**
   - Feeling adventurous? Click this button and let Copilot surprise you with a random feature or tip. Who knows what you might discover?
2. **The "Easter Egg" Commands:**
   - Try typing "Tell me a joke" or "Sing me a song" and see what happens. Copilot has a hidden sense of humor (or at least, it tries).
3. **The "Supercharge" Mode:**
   - If you're looking for truly mind-blowing results, try enabling Copilot's experimental features. These cutting-edge capabilities might not be perfect, but they offer a glimpse into the future of AI assistance.

4. **The "Whisper Network":**
   - Join online communities and forums dedicated to Copilot. You'll find a wealth of tips, tricks, and hidden gems shared by fellow Copilot enthusiasts.
5. **The "Code Whisperer" Mode (for Developers):**
   - If you're a coder, be sure to check out Copilot's code-specific features, like code completion, refactoring suggestions, and documentation generation.

Pro Tips for Gem Hunters:

- **Experiment Fearlessly:** Don't be afraid to try new things and explore Copilot's interface.
- **Read the Release Notes:** Microsoft often sneaks in new features and shortcuts without making a big announcement.
- **Talk to Other Users:** Share your discoveries and learn from others in the Copilot community.

The Thrill of Discovery:

Unearthing Copilot's hidden gems is like finding buried treasure. It's a thrilling experience that can lead to unexpected breakthroughs and newfound productivity. So, grab your pickaxe (or your mouse) and start digging! Who knows what you might find?

Remember: Copilot is constantly evolving, so there are always new gems to be discovered. Keep your eyes peeled, your ears open, and your sense of adventure alive. The world of Copilot is yours to explore!

SECTION B

Copilot in Action: Boosting Productivity Across Applications

CHAPTER SIX

Email Extraordinaire:

Taming the Email Beast with Your AI Wingman

Alright, email fighters, it's time to recover your inbox from the grip of anarchy! We all know the feeling: that sinking dread as you open your email app and see a mountain of unread messages staring back at you. But fear not, because Copilot is here to transform your inbox from a nightmare into a well-oiled machine.

The Inbox Assistant:

Your Personal Email Butler

Copilot isn't just a glorified spellchecker; it's your personal email butler, ready to tackle the tedious tasks that bog you down. Think of it as Alfred Pennyworth to your Batman, handling the mundane details so you can focus on the important stuff.

- **Sorting and Prioritizing:** Copilot can intelligently sort your emails based on sender, subject, or content, ensuring that the most important messages rise to the top. It's like having a personal assistant who knows exactly what to prioritize and what can wait.
- **Drafting Replies:** Struggling to find the right words? Copilot can help you craft professional, concise, and

even witty replies to your emails. It's like having a ghostwriter who knows your voice better than you do.

- **Smart Suggestions:** Copilot can suggest relevant information, attachments, or even follow-up actions based on the content of your emails. It's like having a mind-reader who anticipates your needs before you even know you have them.

Taming the Email Beast:

Tips and Tricks for Inbox Zen

Ready to transform your inbox into a haven of tranquility? Here are a few tips for using Copilot to achieve email nirvana:

- **Train Your AI Butler:** The more you use Copilot, the better it gets at understanding your preferences and communication style. So, don't be afraid to give it feedback and help it learn.
- **Use Keywords and Phrases:** When requesting Copilot to compose a reply, use specific keywords and phrases to guide its response
- . For example, instead of saying "Write a reply," try "Write a polite but firm reply declining this meeting invitation."
- **Embrace the Power of Templates:** Copilot can help you create and save email templates for common responses, saving you time and effort in the long run.

- **Don't Be Afraid to Edit:** Copilot is a powerful tool, but it's not perfect. Always review and edit its suggestions before hitting send.
- **Have Fun!:** Email doesn't have to be a chore. With Copilot by your side, you can inject a little personality and humor into your correspondence.

Beyond the Basics:

Unlocking Copilot's Hidden Email Powers

Copilot's email capabilities go far beyond the basics of sorting, prioritizing, and drafting replies. Here are a few hidden gems to explore:

- **Scheduling Emails:** Ask Copilot to schedule emails for delivery at a later time or date.
- **Generating Meeting Summaries:** Get Copilot to summarize key points and action items from meeting emails.
- **Composing Newsletters:** Use Copilot to brainstorm ideas and draft engaging newsletters for your audience.

The Email Evolution: From Dreaded Chore to Productive Powerhouse

With Copilot's help, email can evolve from a dreaded chore to a powerful tool for communication, collaboration, and productivity. It's time to reclaim your inbox and unleash your email extraordinaire!

Tone It Up (or Down):

From Corporate Stiff to Casual Cool – Copilot's Got Your Back

Forget those bland, robotic emails that sound like they were written by a committee of AI bots. With Copilot, you can inject your emails with personality, flair, and just the right amount of professionalism. Think of it as your digital chameleon, changing its tone to meet your mood, your audience, and your message.

The Tone Spectrum:

Finding Your Email Voice

Email tone is like a spectrum, ranging from ultra-formal (think stuffy corporate jargon) to super-casual (think emojis and LOLs). The trick is finding the right tone for each situation.

- **Formal:** Ideal for business communication, job applications, or when addressing someone you don't know well.
- **Professional:** A safe bet for most workplace communication, striking a balance between formality and approachability.
- **Friendly:** Perfect for colleagues, clients, or anyone you have a good rapport with.
- **Casual:** Best reserved for friends, family, or informal communication.

Copilot's Tone-Shifting Superpowers

The beauty of Copilot is that it can effortlessly switch between these tones, adapting to your needs like a linguistic chameleon. Here's how to unleash its tone-shifting superpowers:

- **Be Explicit:** Tell Copilot exactly what tone you want. "Write a formal email to my boss" or "Draft a casual email to my friend."
- **Use Keywords:** Sprinkle in words that convey your desired tone. For example, "cordial" for a polite tone, "assertive" for a firm tone, or "lighthearted" for a playful tone.
- **Provide Examples:** If you have a specific tone in mind, share an example of an email that embodies that tone.
- **Iterate and Refine:** It's okay to try different things and hone Copilot's recommendations until you get the ideal tone.

- **Examples of Copilot's Tone-Shifting Skills**

Need some inspiration? Here are a few examples of how Copilot can adapt its tone to fit different scenarios:

- **Formal:** "Dear Mr. Smith, I am writing to express my interest in the open position at your company..."
- **Professional:** "Hi James, I hope this email finds you well. I'm following up on our conversation regarding..."

- **Friendly:** "Hey Jane, Just wanted to check in and see how things are going with the project..."
- **Casual:** "Yo dude, What's up? Just wanted to say thanks for the awesome gift..."

The Power of Personality: Injecting Your Unique Flair

Copilot can do more than just mimic different tones; it can also help you inject your unique personality into your emails. By analyzing your writing style and preferences, Copilot can suggest phrases, jokes, or even emojis that align with your personal brand.

So, don't be afraid to let your personality shine through in your emails. With Copilot's help, you can craft messages that are not only effective but also engaging and memorable.

A Word of Caution: Tone It Right, Every Time

While Copilot is great at adapting its tone, it's important to remember that email is a nuanced form of communication. Misinterpreting tone can lead to misunderstandings, hurt feelings, or even damaged relationships.

So, always use your best judgment and double-check Copilot's suggestions before hitting send.

Beyond the Basics:

Unleashing Copilot's Hidden Email Superpowers (Yes, It Can Even Make Coffee... Just Kidding)

Alright, email aficionados, get ready to have your minds blown! Copilot's email prowess extends far beyond the basics of sorting and drafting. We're talking about next-level features that will make you feel like a productivity ninja with a caffeine drip.

Time Travel with Scheduled Emails

Ever wished you could send emails at a specific time, even when you're not around? Well, with Copilot, you can! Just tell it when you want your email to be delivered, and it'll take care of the rest. Perfect for scheduling a follow-up email for when you return from vacation or delivering those "Happy Birthday!" greetings at midnight.

Pro Tip: Use scheduled emails to avoid the dreaded "reply-all" storm when everyone is trying to get their two cents in.

Meeting Summaries: From Mind-Numbing to Mind-Blowing

Let's be honest: most meeting summaries are about as exciting as watching paint dry. But with Copilot, you can transform those mind-numbing notes into a concise, informative, and even (dare we say) entertaining summary.

Copilot can distill the key takeaways, action items, and decisions from your meeting notes, saving you precious time and brainpower. Plus, it can even generate a witty one-liner or two to keep things interesting.

Pro Tip: Use Copilot's meeting summaries to impress your boss or colleagues with your efficiency and attention to detail.

Newsletter Nirvana:

Crafting Engaging Content with Ease

Think writing newsletters is a daunting task? Think again! Copilot can be your creative muse, brainstorming ideas, crafting catchy subject lines, and even generating entire articles. It's like having a team of writers at your fingertips, minus the hefty payroll.

Pro Tip: Experiment with different prompts and tones to find Copilot's sweet spot for newsletter creation. You might be surprised at how creative and engaging its suggestions can be.

Bonus Tip: The Email Concierge

Did you know that Copilot can also help you manage your email subscriptions, unsubscribe from unwanted newsletters, and even track packages? It's like having a personal concierge for your inbox.

The Email Evolution: From Inbox Overload to Inbox Zen

With Copilot's hidden email superpowers, you can finally conquer the email beast and achieve inbox zen. It's time to reclaim your time, boost your productivity, and have a little fun along the way.

Document Dynamo:

Your Co-Author, Brainstorming Buddy, and Grammar Guru (All Rolled into One)

Forget those lonely hours staring at a blank page, wondering where to start. With Copilot as your Document Dynamo, you've got a virtual writing partner who's always ready to spark inspiration, conquer writer's block, and even whip up entire sections of your masterpiece.

The Writing Prompt Whisperer: Banishing Blank Page Syndrome

Writer's block? Meet your new nemesis: Copilot. This AI wordsmith is a master at generating prompts that ignite your creativity and get your ideas flowing. Whether you're struggling to find the perfect opening line or need help brainstorming a blog post outline, Copilot has your back.

Need a catchy headline? Copilot can whip up a dozen options in seconds. Stuck on a plot twist? Let Copilot suggest some unexpected turns of events. It's like having a brainstorming session with your most creative friend, but without the endless chatter and caffeine-fueled tangents.

Structure and Substance:

Building Your Document Brick by Brick

Copilot isn't just about generating ideas; it can also help you structure your document and fill it with substance. Need an outline for your research paper? Copilot can create one in a flash. Want a summary of a lengthy article? Copilot can distill it down to its essence.

But Copilot's document-building powers don't stop there. It can even generate entire sections of text based on your prompts, saving you precious time and energy. Need a product description, a marketing blurb, or even a love letter? Copilot has got you covered.

The Grammar Guru: Polishing Your Prose to Perfection

Even the most seasoned writers make mistakes. That's where Copilot's grammar-checking superpowers come in handy. It can catch typos, grammatical errors, and awkward phrasing, ensuring that your writing is polished and professional.

But Copilot doesn't just point out mistakes; it also suggests improvements. It can help you find the right word, rephrase a clunky sentence, or even restructure a paragraph for better flow and clarity. Think of it as your personal editor, working tirelessly to make your writing shine.

The Creative Collaborator: Your Brainstorming Buddy

Stuck in a creative rut? Copilot can be your brainstorming buddy, bouncing ideas off of you and sparking new connections. Whether you're writing a novel, a screenplay, or a marketing campaign, Copilot can help you think outside the box and explore new possibilities.

Don't be afraid to let your imagination run wild. Copilot is there to catch you if you fall and encourage you to reach for the stars.

Unleash Your Inner Author:

With Copilot as your Document Dynamo, you can unlock your full writing potential and create documents that are not only informative and persuasive but also engaging and enjoyable to read. So, let your creativity flow, and let Copilot be your guide on this literary adventure.

Style Guru: Copilot, Your Personal Grammar Police (But Way More Fun)

Let's be honest: grammar isn't everyone's cup of tea. It's a jungle of rules, exceptions, and confusing jargon that can make even the most seasoned wordsmith break out in a cold sweat. But fear not! Copilot is here to save the day (and your sentence structure).

Polishing Your Prose:

From Drab to Fab

Think of Copilot as your personal writing coach, gently nudging you toward grammatical greatness. It's like having a tiny editor perched on your shoulder, whispering helpful suggestions and correcting your typos before you hit send (or publish).

But Copilot doesn't just catch errors; it elevates your writing to a whole new level. It can suggest more impactful verbs, tighten up your sentences, and even rephrase entire paragraphs for maximum clarity and impact. It's like having a professional wordsmith on speed dial, minus the hefty hourly rate.

Grammar Police: But in a Good Way

Sure, we all have that one friend who's a stickler for grammar (you know, the one who corrects your "your" vs. "you're" usage in casual text messages). But Copilot is like that friend, but way more helpful and less annoying.

It won't judge you for your dangling participles or misplaced modifiers. It'll simply point out the errors and suggest alternatives, all in a friendly, non-judgmental way.

Beyond Grammar: Crafting Compelling Prose

Copilot's language skills go far beyond basic grammar. It can help you:

- **Find the Perfect Word:** Stuck on a word? Ask Copilot for synonyms and antonyms to spice up your vocabulary.
- **Vary Your Sentence Structure:** Tired of short, choppy sentences? Copilot can suggest ways to add variety and rhythm to your writing.

Enhance Your Tone: Want to sound more confident, persuasive, or empathetic? You may adjust your tone to better fit your message with the aid of Copilot.

Real-World Examples:

Copilot's Style Makeovers

Let's see Copilot in action with a few real-world examples:

- **Before:** "The meeting was good, and we talked about a lot of things."
- **After (with Copilot):** "The productive meeting covered a wide range of topics, including next quarter's marketing strategy and budget allocation."
- **Before:** "I am very excited about this opportunity."
- **After (with Copilot):** "I'm thrilled about the opportunity and eager to contribute my skills to the team."
- **Before:** "I think we should not do that."
- **After (with Copilot):** "I recommend against pursuing that course of action due to the potential risks involved."

As you can see, Copilot can transform even the most mundane sentences into clear, concise, and compelling prose.

The Writer's Secret Weapon:

Whether you're a seasoned wordsmith or a casual blogger, Copilot is the ultimate writing tool. It can help you overcome writer's block, polish your prose, and craft messages that resonate with your audience.

So, the next time you're staring at a blank page, don't despair. Just call on your trusty AI sidekick, Copilot, and let the writing magic begin!

Creative Collaborator:

Your Muse, Your Sidekick, Your Partner in (Word) Crime

Move over, muses of ancient Greece! There's a new creative powerhouse in town, and it's not fueled by ambrosia or divine inspiration. It's Copilot, your AI-powered partner in (word) crime, ready to brainstorm, draft, and refine your wildest creative endeavors.

Idea Incubator: Hatching Brilliance with Copilot

Ever felt stuck in a creative rut, staring blankly at a screen, waiting for inspiration to strike? Well, Copilot is your lightning bolt of creativity, ready to jolt your brain into action.

Need a catchy tagline for your new product? Copilot can spit out a dozen options in seconds. Struggling to come up with a compelling hook for your novel? Allow Copilot to make some surprising turns and suggestions.

From blog post topics to social media captions, Copilot is a wellspring of ideas, always ready to spark your imagination.

Storytelling Sorcerer: Crafting Worlds with Words

Whether you're a seasoned novelist or a budding screenwriter, Copilot can help you weave captivating stories that transport readers to other worlds.

Need help developing a character? Copilot can offer insights into their personality, motivations, and backstory. Struggling with dialogue? Let Copilot suggest snappy exchanges that crackle with wit and authenticity. From plot outlines to scene descriptions, Copilot can help you bring your story to life.

Marketing Maverick:

Crafting Compelling Copy That Converts

In the cutthroat world of marketing, every word counts. That's where Copilot comes in. This AI-powered wordsmith can help you craft persuasive copy that grabs attention, sparks interest, and drives action.

Need a killer headline for your landing page? Copilot can conjure up a dozen options that are sure to convert. Want to create a social media campaign that goes viral? Let Copilot brainstorm catchy slogans and hashtags that resonate with your audience. From product descriptions to email campaigns, Copilot is your secret weapon for marketing success.

Real-World Examples: Copilot's Creative Collaborations

Don't believe us? Here are a few real-world examples of how Copilot has helped creatives:

- **Author:** Co-authored a science fiction novel with Copilot, blending human imagination with AI-generated ideas.
- **Screenwriter:** Developed a screenplay with Copilot, using its suggestions to create compelling dialogue and plot twists.

- **Marketing Manager:** Generated a successful social media campaign with Copilot's help, resulting in increased brand awareness and engagement.

The Creative Playground: Where Imagination Meets Innovation

Copilot is more than just a tool; it's a playground for your imagination, a place where you can experiment, explore, and push the boundaries of creativity. With Copilot by your side, there's no limit to what you can achieve.

So, unleash your inner artist, embrace the power of AI, and let Copilot be your creative collaborator on your next project. Who knows what masterpieces you might create together?

Social Media Savvy:

Your AI Hype Squad for Likes, Shares, and Viral Glory

Tired of staring at a blank social media post, wondering how to capture your audience's attention in a sea of cat videos and political rants? Fear not, my fellow content creators, because Copilot is your secret weapon for social media domination. Think of it as your personal hype squad, ready to brainstorm, draft, and refine posts that will make your followers double-tap with glee.

Post Perfect: Crafting Engaging Content That Cuts Through the Noise

Let's face it: social media is a battlefield for attention. But with Copilot in your corner, you can create posts that stand out from the crowd, spark conversations, and leave your competitors green with envy.

Need a witty caption for your latest Instagram photo? Copilot can conjure up a dozen options in seconds, each one more clever than the last. Want to write a Facebook post that gets people talking? Let Copilot help you craft a thought-provoking question or a controversial statement that's sure to generate buzz.

But Copilot isn't just about cleverness. It can also help you tailor your posts to specific platforms and audiences. Whether you're tweeting for Twitter, posting on LinkedIn, or creating a TikTok video, Copilot can help you find the right voice and tone for each channel.

Caption Connoisseur: Adding Spice to Your Visuals

While an image may be worth a thousand words, it may become much more valuable with a clever description.

Copilot is a master of the one-liner, crafting captions that are not only informative but also funny, relatable, or thought-provoking.

Need a caption for your vacation photo that doesn't just say "Wish you were here"? Copilot can assist you in creating a clever comment that encapsulates your experience.

Want to add some humor to your latest product shot? Let Copilot suggest a pun or a pop culture reference that will make your followers chuckle.

Ad Copy Ace:

Turning Clicks into Customers

Advertising on social media is an effective strategy for expanding one's clientele and increasing revenue.

But crafting effective ad copy is an art form in itself. That's where Copilot comes in.

This AI-powered wordsmith can help you create ad copy that's not only attention-grabbing but also persuasive and results-oriented. It can suggest compelling headlines, powerful calls to action, and even A/B test different versions of your ad copy to see what works best.

Real-World Examples: Copilot's Social Media Success Stories

Don't just take our word for it. Copilot has already helped countless businesses and individuals achieve social media success.

- **Small Business Owner:** Increased engagement and followers by using Copilot to craft witty and relatable social media posts.
- **Influencer:** Boosted their reach and engagement by using Copilot to create viral TikTok videos.
- **Marketing Agency:** Achieved impressive results for their clients by using Copilot to generate targeted ad copy that converted.

The Social Media Evolution: From Follower to Influencer (with a Little Help from Your AI Friend)

With Copilot as your social media sidekick, you can transform your online presence from follower to influencer. It's time to unleash your creativity, connect with your audience, and build a community of loyal fans.

So, what are you waiting for? Let Copilot lead the way as you embark on your social media journey.

Together, you can create content that not only entertains and informs but also inspires and empowers.

Blog Booster:

Your AI Muse for Content That Clicks, Converts, and Keeps Readers Coming Back for More

Let's be honest: blogging can be a grind. Between brainstorming topics, outlining your thoughts, and actually writing the darn thing, it's enough to make even the most passionate wordsmith want to throw their laptop out the window. But fear not, weary bloggers, because Copilot is here to transform your blogging experience from a slog to a sprint.

Idea Factory: From Blank Page to Brilliant Concepts

Writer's block? Not on Copilot's watch! This AI idea generator is like a caffeine-fueled brainstorming session, churning out blog post ideas faster than you can say "content calendar."

Simply give Copilot a broad topic or keyword, and watch as it conjures up a list of captivating blog post titles, angles, and even full-fledged outlines. It's like having a team of content strategists working tirelessly in the background, ensuring you never run out of fresh ideas.

Outline Oracle: Structuring Your Thoughts Like a Pro

Once you've settled on a topic, Copilot can help you structure your thoughts and create a well-organized outline. It can suggest logical sections, subheadings, and even specific points to cover in each section. It's like having a personal writing coach who knows exactly how to turn your scattered thoughts into a cohesive masterpiece.

The Drafting Dynamo: From Outline to Article in a Flash

But Copilot doesn't stop at outlines. It can also help you draft entire articles based on your chosen topic and outline. It's like having a ghostwriter who's always on call, ready to churn out high-quality content at a moment's notice.

Of course, Copilot isn't perfect. Its writing might need a bit of polishing and editing, but it's a fantastic starting point that can save you hours of work and mental energy.

Real-World Results: Bloggers Raving About Copilot

Don't just take our word for it. Copilot has already helped countless bloggers boost their traffic, engagement, and even revenue.

- **Freelance Writer:** Increased their monthly income by using Copilot to generate more high-quality content in less time.
- **Small Business Owner:** Attracted new customers and leads by using Copilot to create engaging blog posts that rank well in search engines.
- **Hobby Blogger:** Rediscovered their passion for writing by using Copilot to overcome writer's block and consistently publish new content.

The Blogosphere's Best-Kept Secret:

Copilot is quickly becoming the blogosphere's best-kept secret, empowering writers of all levels to create content that resonates with their audience and drives results.

Whether you're a seasoned blogger or a newbie just starting, Copilot can help you take your writing to the next level. So, ditch the writer's block, embrace the power of AI, and let Copilot be your blogging muse!

Pro Tips for Blogging with Copilot:

- **Provide Clear Prompts:** The more specific your instructions, the better Copilot can tailor its suggestions to your needs.
- **Experiment with Different Styles:** Copilot can mimic different writing styles, from formal to casual to humorous. Find the voice that best suits your brand.

- **Edit and Refine:** Copilot's writing is a starting point, not a finished product. Always review and edit its suggestions before publishing.
- **Use Copilot for Inspiration, Not Plagiarism:** Copilot is a tool, not a replacement for your own creativity. Use its suggestions as a springboard for your own ideas.

Presentation Pro:

Your AI Co-Pilot for Slide Deck Stardom (No Boring Bullet Points Allowed!)

Say goodbye to death by PowerPoint and hello to standing ovations! With Copilot as your Presentation Pro, you'll be crafting slide decks that not only inform but also captivate and inspire. No more soul-crushing bullet points or clip art from the 90s. We're talking about presentations that are so good, your audience might actually stay awake.

Slide Show Superstar: Designing Decks That Dazzle

Copilot isn't just about words; it's also a design whiz. It can help you create visually appealing slide layouts, suggest complementary color schemes, and even whip up custom graphics. Think of it as your personal design consultant, minus the pretentious beret and oversized glasses.

But Copilot's design skills go beyond aesthetics. It can also help you organize your content in a way that's easy to follow and visually engaging. No more endless bullet points or walls of text. With Copilot, your slides will be clean, concise, and impactful.

Content Creator Extraordinaire:

From Blank Slides to Brilliant Ideas

Staring at a blank slide can be more terrifying than public speaking itself. But fear not, because Copilot is your brainstorming buddy, ready to fill those empty spaces with brilliant ideas.

Need a catchy opening line? Copilot can suggest a few options that will hook your audience from the get-go. Want to summarize complex data in a way that's easy to understand? Let Copilot transform those numbers into a compelling story. From attention-grabbing headlines to thought-provoking questions, Copilot is your creative muse for slide content.

Speaker Notes Whisperer: Your Secret Weapon for Smooth Delivery

Even the most seasoned presenters need a little help sometimes. That's where Copilot's speaker notes come in. These handy prompts can help you stay on track, remember key points, and deliver your presentation with confidence and charisma.

But Copilot's speaker notes aren't just a crutch; they're a secret weapon. They can help you anticipate audience questions, inject humor into your talk, and even suggest ways to engage your listeners.

Real-World Raves: Copilot's Presentation Prowess in Action

Don't just take our word for it. Copilot has already helped countless professionals deliver presentations that wowed their audiences.

- **CEO:** Secured funding for a new venture with a Copilot-powered pitch deck that blew away investors.
- **Salesperson:** Closed a major deal after using Copilot to create a persuasive sales presentation that highlighted the product's key benefits.
- **Educator:** Engaged students and improved learning outcomes by using Copilot to create interactive and visually appealing presentations.

From Nervous Presenter to Polished Pro:

With Copilot as your presentation pro, you can transform your next talk from a nerve-wracking ordeal into a show-stopping performance. It's time to ditch the boring bullet points, embrace the power of AI, and become the presentation rockstar you were born to be.

CHAPTER SEVEN

Code Whisperer:

Your AI Pair Programmer (Who Never Hogs the Keyboard)

Alright, coding wizards and aspiring software sorcerers, get ready to meet your new best friend: Copilot, the AI-powered coding companion that's about to make your life a whole lot easier (and your code a whole lot cleaner).

Autocomplete Ace: Your Coding Crystal Ball

Ever wished you had a crystal ball that could predict your next line of code? Well, Copilot is the next best thing. This autocomplete ace can anticipate your coding intentions, suggest relevant snippets, functions, and even entire blocks of code. It's like having a mind-reading partner who's always one step ahead of you.

But Copilot isn't just about saving you keystrokes; it's about boosting your productivity, improving your code quality, and helping you learn new programming languages and techniques. It's like having a seasoned mentor who's always there to offer guidance and support.

The Magic of Contextual Awareness

Copilot's autocomplete magic isn't just based on guesswork; it's powered by a deep understanding of your codebase and the context of your current task. It analyzes your code, your comments, and even your variable names to provide suggestions that are both relevant and accurate.

This contextual awareness is what sets Copilot apart from other autocomplete tools. It's not just regurgitating common code patterns; it's understanding the unique nuances of your project and offering tailored suggestions that fit seamlessly into your workflow.

Real-World Examples: Copilot's Autocomplete Awesomeness

Don't just take our word for it. Copilot's autocomplete capabilities have already revolutionized the way developers write code.

- **The Python Pro:** Saved hours of typing by using Copilot to generate boilerplate code, import statements, and common functions.
- **The JavaScript Jedi:** Learned new JavaScript libraries and frameworks faster than ever, thanks to Copilot's intelligent suggestions.
- **The Coding Newbie:** Gained confidence and momentum in their coding journey, with Copilot acting as a helpful guide and mentor.

Beyond Autocomplete: A Coding Companion for All Seasons

Copilot's code completion capabilities are just the tip of the iceberg. This versatile AI sidekick can also help you:

- **Debug Your Code:** Identify errors, suggest fixes, and explain complex code logic.
- **Refactor Your Code:** Improve code structure, efficiency, and readability.
- **Generate Documentation:** Create clear and concise code comments and documentation.
- **Explore New Languages:** Learn new programming languages and frameworks with ease.

Unleash Your Inner Coding Genius:

With Copilot as your coding companion, you can unlock your full potential and achieve coding greatness. So, fire up your code editor, let Copilot take the wheel (or at least the keyboard), and get ready to experience the future of coding.

Debugging Dynamo:

Your AI Exterminator for Pesky Bugs (No Bug Spray Required!)

Let's face it: debugging code can be a real buzzkill. It's like trying to find a needle in a haystack, except the needle is a tiny typo and the haystack is a thousand lines of code. But fear not, weary coders, because Copilot is here to rescue you from the depths of debugging despair.

The Bug Exterminator: Zapping Errors with Laser-Focused Precision

Copilot is like a bug exterminator with X-ray vision, laser-focused on identifying and eliminating those pesky errors that plague your code. It can spot syntax errors, logical flaws, and even potential performance bottlenecks.

But Copilot doesn't just point out the problem; it offers solutions. It can suggest fixes, refactor your code, and even explain the underlying logic, helping you learn from your mistakes and become a better programmer in the process.

The Code Whisperer's Diagnostic Skills

Copilot's debugging prowess is powered by its deep understanding of code and its ability to analyze complex patterns. It's like having a seasoned developer peer over your shoulder, offering insights and guidance based on years of experience.

But Copilot doesn't just rely on its own knowledge. It also taps into a vast network of code repositories and online resources, drawing on the collective wisdom of the programming community to provide the most accurate and up-to-date solutions.

Real-World Examples: Copilot's Debugging Triumphs

Don't just take our word for it. Copilot has already saved countless developers from the brink of coding despair.

- **The Junior Developer:** Fixed a frustrating bug that had been plaguing their code for days, thanks to Copilot's insightful suggestions.
- **The Seasoned Pro:** Discovered a hidden performance bottleneck that was slowing down their application, with Copilot's help.
- **The Open Source Contributor:** Improved the code quality of a popular project by using Copilot to identify and fix errors.

Beyond Debugging: A Code Therapist for Your Soul

Copilot isn't just about fixing bugs; it's about helping you understand your code and become a better programmer. It's like having a code therapist who can explain complex concepts in simple terms, offer encouragement when you're feeling stuck, and celebrate your victories with you.

Unleash Your Inner Debugging Guru:

With Copilot as your debugging dynamo, you can spend less time wrestling with errors and more time building amazing software. Thus, embrace AI's potential, bid bugs farewell, and look forward to a more productive and pleasurable coding experience.

Pro Tips for Debugging with Copilot:

- **Provide Context:** The more information you give Copilot about your code and the problem you're facing, the better it can help you.

- **Ask Specific Questions:** Instead of saying "My code is broken," try "I'm getting an error message on line 25. Can you help me understand what's happening?"
- **Experiment with Different Prompts:** Copilot can offer different types of debugging assistance. Try experimenting with different prompts to see what works best for you.
- **Don't Be Afraid to Ask for Help:** If Copilot can't solve your problem, don't hesitate to reach out to online communities or forums for additional support.

With Copilot by your side, you'll be debugging like a pro in no time. So, go forth and conquer those pesky bugs!

Language Learner:

Your Babel Fish for Code (No Hitchhiking Across the Galaxy Required!)

Copilot is like the Babel Fish for code, helping you navigate the vast and sometimes confusing landscape of programming languages. Whether you're dabbling in Python, exploring JavaScript, or venturing into the wilds of C++, Copilot can be your trusty translator, breaking down language barriers and helping you speak fluent code in no time.

The Multilingual Marvel: Breaking Down Language Barriers

Programming languages are like dialects of a global coding culture. Each language has its own syntax, quirks, and idioms, and it can be daunting to switch between them. But with Copilot by your side, you don't need to be a polyglot programmer to understand and work with different languages.

Copilot's language learning capabilities are truly impressive. It can not only translate code snippets between languages but also explain the logic behind the code and offer suggestions for improving it. It's like having a personal tutor who's fluent in every programming language under the sun.

Code Translation: From Python to Java (and Everything In Between)

Need to convert a Python script into Java? No problem! Copilot can do it in a snap. Want to translate a C++ function into JavaScript? Easy peasy! Copilot has got you covered.

But Copilot's translation skills aren't just about syntax conversion. It also understands the nuances of each language, ensuring that the translated code is idiomatic, efficient, and maintainable. It's like having a professional translator who's also a seasoned software engineer.

Beyond Translation: A Language Learning Companion

Copilot isn't just a translator; it's also a language learning companion. It can help you:

Learn New Languages: With the help of Copilot's insightful recommendations and code samples, you can easily explore new programming languages and frameworks.

- **Understand Code Logic:** Get clear explanations of complex code snippets, regardless of the language.
- **Improve Your Code:** Learn best practices and coding conventions for different languages.

Real-World Examples: Copilot's Language Learning Prowess

Don't just take our word for it. Copilot has already helped countless developers expand their linguistic repertoire and conquer new coding challenges.

- **The Web Developer:** Successfully transitioned from front-end development to back-end development by using Copilot to learn new languages like Node.js and Python.
- **The Data Scientist:** Leveraged Copilot to quickly learn and apply R, a statistical programming language, to their data analysis projects.
- **The Student:** Got a head start in their computer science course by using Copilot to practice coding in multiple languages.

Your Passport to Multilingual Coding:

With Copilot as your language learner, you can break down language barriers, explore new horizons, and become a truly polyglot programmer. So, dust off your passport, pack your bags, and let's embark on an exciting coding adventure around the world of programming languages!

Pro Tips for Language Learning with Copilot:

- **Be Specific:** Tell Copilot which languages you want to translate between or learn more about.
- **Provide Context:** The more context you give Copilot about your code and its purpose, the more accurate its translations and suggestions will be.
- **Ask for Explanations:** Don't just ask Copilot to translate code; ask it to explain the logic behind the code as well.
- **Practice, Practice, Practice:** The more you use Copilot for language learning, the better it will get at understanding your needs and providing tailored suggestions.

Refactoring Refresher: Copilot, Your Code's Personal Trainer (No Sweatbands Required!)

Think of your code as a finely tuned athlete, capable of amazing feats of speed and agility. But even the most elite athletes need a little coaching and fine-tuning from time to time. That's where Copilot comes in, your code's personal trainer, ready to whip your messy spaghetti code into shape and turn it into a lean, mean, bug-free machine.

The Art of Refactoring: It's Not Just Spring Cleaning, It's Code Optimization

Refactoring isn't just about tidying up your code; it's about improving its structure, readability, and efficiency. Think of it as giving your code a spa day: a little pampering here, a little polishing there, and before you know it, your code is looking and feeling its best.

But unlike a spa day, refactoring isn't just about appearances. It's about enhancing your code's performance, reducing errors, and making it easier to maintain and update. It's like upgrading from a clunker to a sports car – you get a smoother ride, better gas mileage, and a whole lot more fun.

Copilot, the Refactoring Guru:

Copilot isn't just a code completion tool; it's also a refactoring guru. It can analyze your code, identify areas for improvement, and suggest refactorings that can make your code cleaner, faster, and more efficient. It's like having a seasoned developer peer over your shoulder, offering expert advice on how to optimize your codebase.

But Copilot doesn't just offer suggestions; it can also do the heavy lifting for you. It can automatically refactor your code, making complex changes with just a few clicks (or a single voice command). It's like having a team of code monkeys at your disposal, ready to tackle the most tedious refactoring tasks.

Real-World Examples: Copilot's Refactoring Victories

Don't just take our word for it. Copilot has already helped countless developers transform their code from messy to magnificent.

- **The Startup Founder:** Refactored their codebase to improve performance and scalability, allowing their company to handle rapid growth.
- **The Open Source Maintainer:** Made their project more accessible to new contributors by refactoring the code to follow best practices and coding conventions.
- **The Solo Developer:** Saved countless hours of debugging and maintenance by using Copilot to identify and fix code smells before they became major problems.

Beyond Refactoring: A Holistic Approach to Code Health

Copilot's refactoring capabilities are just one part of its arsenal of code improvement tools. It can also help you:

- **Write Cleaner Code:** Suggest better variable names, function names, and code formatting.
- **Identify Potential Bugs:** Spot common coding errors and suggest fixes.
- **Generate Tests:** Create unit tests to ensure your code is working as expected.

Transform Your Code into a Masterpiece:

With Copilot as your refactoring guru, you can turn your code into a work of art. It's time to say goodbye to messy spaghetti code and hello to clean, efficient, and maintainable code that you can be proud of.

Pro Tips for Refactoring with Copilot:

Start Small: Don't try to refactor your entire codebase at once. Concentrate on making little, gradual adjustments that are simple to test and validate.

- **Test Thoroughly:** After each refactoring, be sure to run your tests to ensure that your code still works as expected.
- **Don't Be Afraid to Ask for Help:** If you're not sure how to refactor a particular piece of code, don't hesitate to ask Copilot for suggestions or consult with other developers.
- **Embrace the Process:** Refactoring is a continuous process as opposed to a single action. As your code evolves, so should your refactoring efforts.

With Copilot by your side, you'll be refactoring like a pro in no time. So, grab your virtual dumbbells and get ready to transform your code into a lean, mean, bug-free machine!

Documentation Dynamo:

Your AI Scribe for Code Comments That Don't Make You Cringe (or Cry)

Let's be honest: writing code documentation can be about as exciting as watching a compiler churn through a thousand lines of code (yawn). But it's a necessary evil, essential for understanding, maintaining, and collaborating on complex projects. Thankfully, Copilot is here to rescue you from the drudgery of documenting your code.

The Scribe of Silicon Valley: Making Sense of Your Spaghetti Code

Copilot isn't just a code completion wizard; it's also a documentation dynamo. It can analyze your code, understand its purpose and functionality, and generate clear, concise comments and documentation that actually make sense. No more cryptic abbreviations, outdated explanations, or inside jokes that only you understand. Copilot helps you create documentation that's informative, accessible, and (dare we say) even enjoyable to read.

From Cryptic Comments to Crystal-Clear Explanations

Remember those code comments that left you scratching your head, wondering what the heck the original developer was thinking? Well, Copilot can help you avoid that fate. It can generate comments that explain the purpose of your code, the logic behind it, and any potential gotchas or edge cases. It's like having a seasoned developer whispering in your ear, guiding you through the intricacies of your codebase.

Documentation Made Easy (and Even a Little Fun)

Copilot takes the pain out of writing documentation by automating the tedious parts. It can:

- **Generate Function and Variable Descriptions:** Explain what each piece of code does and how it fits into the overall project.
- **Document Code Logic:** Describe the flow of control, decision points, and error handling in your code.
- **Create API Documentation:** Generate comprehensive documentation for your APIs, making it easy for other developers to use your code.

Real-World Examples: Copilot's Documentation Prowess

Don't just take our word for it. Copilot has already helped countless developers create documentation that's not only informative but also a joy to read.

- **The Open Source Guru:** Improved the documentation of their popular project, making it easier for new contributors to understand and contribute to the codebase.
- **The Enterprise Architect:** Created comprehensive documentation for their company's internal APIs,

streamlining collaboration and reducing onboarding time for new developers.

- **The Solo Developer:** Saved countless hours of frustration by using Copilot to generate clear and concise code comments.

The Documentation Dream Team: You and Copilot

With Copilot as your documentation dynamo, you can create code that's not only functional but also well-documented and easy to understand. It's a win-win for everyone involved:

- **You:** Spend less time on documentation and more time on coding.
- **Your Teammates:** Can easily understand and work with your code.
- **Future You:** Will thank you when you revisit your code months or even years later.

Pro Tips for Documenting Your Code with Copilot:

- **Start Early:** Don't wait until the end of your project to start documenting your code. Start early and document as you go.
- **Be Consistent:** When writing comments and documenting, use a standard structure and style.
- **Keep It Concise:** Don't write novels in your code comments. Keep it simple, pleasant, and straightforward.

- **Use Copilot's Suggestions as a Starting Point:** Copilot's suggestions are a great starting point, but don't be afraid to edit and refine them to fit your specific needs.

With Copilot by your side, you can transform your code documentation from a chore into a breeze. So, unleash your inner scribe, and let Copilot help you create code that's not only functional but also well-documented and easy to understand.

Testing Titan:

Your AI Quality Assurance Squad (Minus the Clipboards and Lab Coats)

Forget those tedious hours of manual testing and endless debugging sessions. With Copilot as your Testing Titan, you'll be squashing bugs, identifying edge cases, and ensuring code quality like a seasoned QA pro. It's like having a whole team of testers at your disposal, minus the endless meetings and stale donuts.

Test Case Creator Extraordinaire: Generating Test Cases with a Click

Writing test cases can be a real drag. But with Copilot, it's as easy as pie (or maybe even easier, depending on your baking skills). Simply provide Copilot with a description of your code's functionality, and it will generate a comprehensive set of test cases that cover a wide range of scenarios.

No more agonizing over edge cases or trying to remember every possible input combination. Copilot has got you covered, freeing you up to focus on more important things, like actually writing the code.

Bug Hunter: Finding Flaws Before They Find You

Copilot isn't just about writing test cases; it's also a master bug hunter. By analyzing your code and running your test cases, it can identify potential bugs and vulnerabilities before they wreak havoc on your application.

Think of it as a proactive security system for your code, constantly scanning for weaknesses and alerting you to potential threats. It's like having a trusty watchdog who's always on the lookout for intruders.

Code Quality Guardian: Ensuring Your Code is Top-Notch

Code quality is more than just the absence of bugs; it's about creating code that's readable, maintainable, and scalable. Copilot can help you achieve these goals by suggesting improvements to your code structure, formatting, and naming conventions.

It's like having a personal code reviewer who's always available to offer constructive feedback and help you elevate your code to the next level.

Real-World Examples: Copilot's Testing Triumphs

Don't just take our word for it. Copilot has already helped countless developers improve their code quality and reduce bugs.

- **The Agile Team:** Streamlined their testing process and reduced time to market by using Copilot to generate and execute test cases.
- **The Solo Developer:** Improved the reliability of their code by catching and fixing bugs early on with Copilot's help.
- **The Open Source Community:** Enhanced the quality of their project by using Copilot to identify and address code smells and vulnerabilities.

The Testing Transformation: From Tedious to Terrific

With Copilot as your Testing Titan, you can transform the way you test your code. It's time to say goodbye to tedious manual testing and hello to a streamlined, automated, and enjoyable testing experience.

Pro Tips for Testing with Copilot:

- **Write Testable Code:** Structure your code in a way that makes it easy to test.
- **Start Early:** Don't wait until the end of your project to start writing tests. Start early then test as you go.

- **Use Copilot's Suggestions:** Don't be afraid to let Copilot generate test cases and suggest refactorings.
- **Review and Refine:** Always review Copilot's suggestions and make sure they're accurate and relevant to your code.

You will quickly become a testing titan with Copilot at your side. So, put on your cape (optional) and get ready to conquer the world of software testing!

Beyond Code:

Project Planning Pro: Your AI Project Manager (Minus the Nagging Reminders)

Alright, fellow project wranglers, buckle up! We're about to venture beyond the realm of code and into the wild world of project management. But don't worry, this isn't your grandma's Gantt chart. With Copilot as your Project Planning Pro, you'll be orchestrating projects like a seasoned conductor, minus the baton twirling (unless you're into that sort of thing).

The Project Planning Guru: From Chaos to Clarity

Let's be honest: most project plans start out as a chaotic mess of ideas, deadlines, and to-do lists scribbled on random scraps of paper. But with Copilot's help, you can transform that chaos into a beautifully organized project plan that even your most OCD colleague would approve of.

Need help outlining project goals and objectives? Copilot can brainstorm with you, ensuring you're aligned with your stakeholders and on track to achieve your desired outcomes.

Struggling to create a realistic timeline? Copilot can help you estimate task durations, identify dependencies, and build a schedule that actually works.

The Taskmaster: Wrangling To-Dos with AI Precision

To-do lists are the bane of every project manager's existence. They're constantly growing, shifting, and threatening to overwhelm you. But with Copilot as your Taskmaster, you can tame those unruly to-dos and keep your project on track.

Copilot can help you break down complex tasks into smaller, more manageable chunks, assign tasks to team members, and even track progress in real-time. It's like having a personal assistant who's always on top of your to-do list, ensuring that nothing falls through the cracks.

Real-World Examples: Copilot's Project Planning Prowess

Don't just take our word for it. Copilot has already helped countless teams deliver projects on time and under budget.

- **The Marketing Team:** Launched a successful product launch campaign with Copilot's help, hitting all their milestones and exceeding their goals.
- **The Software Development Team:** Delivered a complex software project on time and under budget, thanks to Copilot's ability to identify and resolve potential roadblocks early on.

- **The Non-Profit Organization:** Streamlined their grant application process and secured funding for a new initiative, with Copilot's help.

The Project Planning Revolution: From Headaches to High-Fives

With Copilot as your project planning pro, you can transform your project management experience from a headache-inducing ordeal to a collaborative and enjoyable process. It's time to ditch the stress, embrace the power of AI, and start celebrating your project successes.

Pro Tips for Project Planning with Copilot:

- **Define Your Goals Clearly:** Before you start planning, make sure you have a clear understanding of your project goals and objectives.
- **Break Down Tasks into Manageable Chunks:** Don't try to tackle everything at once. Divide the work involved in your project into smaller, more doable chunks.
- **Use Copilot's Suggestions:** Don't be afraid to let Copilot generate project outlines, timelines, and task lists.
- **Communicate Effectively:** Keep your team updated on progress and any changes to the project plan.
- **Celebrate Successes:** Don't forget to celebrate your team's achievements along the way.

With Copilot by your side, you'll be a project planning pro in no time. So, grab your virtual hard hat and get ready to build some amazing things!

Code Review Companion:

Your AI Sidekick for Code That's Clean, Mean, and Bug-Free

Picture this: You've just finished a marathon coding session, your eyes are bleary, and your brain is fried. The last thing you want to do is scrutinize your code for errors and potential improvements. Enter Copilot, your virtual code review companion, ready to lend a fresh set of eyes (and a healthy dose of AI-powered analysis) to your masterpiece.

The Code Whisperer's Second Opinion: An Objective Perspective on Your Code

Copilot isn't just a code completion tool; it's also a seasoned code reviewer. It can analyze your code, identify potential issues, and suggest improvements, all without the ego or personal biases that sometimes come with human feedback.

Think of it as a second opinion from a trusted colleague, but without the awkwardness of asking someone to critique your work. Copilot offers objective, unbiased feedback that can help you catch errors, improve readability, and optimize performance.

Spotting Bugs and Code Smells: Copilot's X-Ray Vision

Copilot has a keen eye for spotting bugs and code smells—those subtle hints of potential problems that can snowball into major headaches down the road. It can identify issues like:

- **Syntax Errors:** Missing semicolons, typos, and other grammatical slip-ups.
- **Logical Errors:** Incorrect algorithms, infinite loops, and other flaws in your code's reasoning.
- **Performance Bottlenecks:** Inefficient code that slows down your application.
- **Security Vulnerabilities:** Potential entry points for hackers and other malicious actors.

Beyond Bug Hunting: Moving Your Code to the Next Level

Copilot doesn't just point out problems; it offers solutions. It can suggest alternative implementations, recommend best practices, and even refactor your code to make it cleaner, more efficient, and easier to maintain.

It's like having a coding mentor who's always available to offer guidance and support, helping you level up your skills and write better code.

Real-World Examples: Copilot's Code Review Wins

Don't just take our word for it. Copilot has already helped countless developers improve their code quality and catch errors before they cause problems.

- **The Junior Developer:** Learned from their mistakes and improved their coding skills, thanks to Copilot's constructive feedback.
- **The Senior Developer:** Saved time and energy by automating repetitive code review tasks, allowing them to focus on more complex challenges.
- **The Open Source Project:** Improved code quality and collaboration by using Copilot to streamline their code review process.

Your Virtual Code Review Partner:

With Copilot as your code review companion, you can write code that's not only functional but also clean, efficient, and maintainable. It's a win-win for everyone involved:

- **You:** Get immediate feedback on your code, catch errors early on, and improve your coding skills.
- **Your Teammates:** Benefit from cleaner, more reliable code that's easier to understand and collaborate on.
- **Your Users:** Enjoy a better user experience thanks to more stable and performant software.

Pro Tips for Code Review with Copilot:

- **Be Open to Feedback:** Don't take Copilot's suggestions personally. Remember, it's just trying to help you write better code.
- **Ask for Clarification:** If you don't understand a suggestion, ask Copilot for more information or an explanation.
- **Experiment with Different Settings:** Copilot's code review capabilities can be customized to your preferences. Try out several configurations to see what suits you the best.

With Copilot by your side, you'll be a code review ninja in no time. So, embrace the power of AI, say goodbye to code smells, and hello to code that's clean, mean, and bug-free!

CHAPTER EIGHT

Spreadsheet Sorcerer:

Taming Excel's Wild Formulas with Your AI Spellbook (No Magic Wand Required, But It Couldn't Hurt)

Alright, number crunchers and spreadsheet aficionados, get ready to level up your Excel game! If you've ever felt lost in a labyrinth of formulas, functions, and cryptic calculations, Copilot is here to be your trusty guide. Think of it as your personal Excel wizard, armed with a spellbook of knowledge and a knack for turning complex formulas into simple incantations.

Formula Wizard: Your Excel Spellbook

Excel formulas can be a real head-scratcher. They're like a secret language with its own syntax, rules, and quirks. But with Copilot as your formula wizard, you can unlock the secrets of Excel and create complex calculations with ease.

Need to calculate a weighted average, a VLOOKUP, or even a nested IF statement? Just ask Copilot, and it'll conjure up the perfect formula for you. No more poring over documentation or searching online forums for help. Copilot is your one-stop shop for Excel expertise.

Complex Calculations Made Easy:

Copilot isn't just about simple formulas; it can handle even the most complex calculations. Need to analyze a massive dataset, build a financial model, or create a custom report? Copilot can help you do it all, without breaking a sweat.

Think of it as your personal Excel tutor, guiding you through the process step-by-step and explaining the logic behind each formula. With Copilot by your side, you'll be a spreadsheet sorcerer in no time.

Real-World Examples: Copilot's Formula Wizardry in Action

Don't just take our word for it. Copilot has already helped countless Excel users conquer their spreadsheet challenges.

- **The Finance Analyst:** Streamlined their financial modeling process and reduced errors with Copilot's help.
- **The Marketing Manager:** Analyzed customer data and identified key trends with Copilot's powerful formulas and functions.
- **The Small Business Owner:** Created custom invoices and reports with ease, thanks to Copilot's expertise.

Beyond Formulas: Excel's Hidden Powers

Copilot's formula wizardry is just one aspect of its Excel superpowers. It can also help you:

- **Automate Tasks:** Use Copilot to create macros and automate repetitive tasks, saving you time and effort.
- **Create Custom Functions:** Build your own personalized functions to meet your specific needs.
- **Integrate with Other Tools:** Connect Copilot with other data sources and applications to unlock even more powerful insights.

From Excel Novice to Spreadsheet Sorcerer:

With Copilot as your guide, you can unlock the full potential of Excel and become a spreadsheet sorcerer. Now prepare to take on the realm of data analysis by donning your wizard hat (optional)!

Pro Tips for Excel Mastery with Copilot:

- **Be Specific:** When asking Copilot for help with a formula, be as specific as possible about what you're trying to achieve.
- **Experiment:** Don't be afraid to try different formulas and functions. Copilot can help you find the best solution for your needs.
- **Learn from the Master:** Use Copilot as a learning tool. Pay attention to the formulas it suggests and the explanations it provides.
- **Have Fun:** Excel doesn't have to be boring. With Copilot, you can make it fun and even a little bit magical!

With Copilot by your side, you'll be casting Excel spells like a pro in no time. So, grab your wand (or your mouse) and let the spreadsheet sorcery begin!

Data Detective:

Uncover Hidden Insights in Your Data with Copilot's Sleuthing Skills (Magnifying Glass Not Included)

Attention all data detectives and spreadsheet sleuths! Prepare to ditch your magnifying glass and dust for fingerprints because Copilot is here to revolutionize your data analysis game. With Copilot as your trusty sidekick, you'll be uncovering hidden trends, spotting sneaky outliers, and transforming raw data into actionable insights faster than Sherlock Holmes on a caffeine binge.

Unmasking Hidden Patterns: Your Data's Secret Decoder Ring

Data analysis can often feel like staring at a wall of numbers, trying to decipher hidden messages. But Copilot is your secret decoder ring, revealing patterns and trends that would otherwise remain hidden in plain sight.

Whether you're analyzing sales figures, customer behavior, or scientific data, Copilot can help you identify patterns that can inform your decision-making, improve your strategies, and give you a competitive edge. It's like having a data whisperer who can translate the language of numbers into actionable insights.

Outlier Alert: Spotting the Unusual Suspects

Outliers are the black sheep of the data world - those unusual data points that don't seem to fit in with the rest of the flock.

But outliers can be valuable clues, pointing to potential errors, anomalies, or even groundbreaking discoveries.

Copilot is your outlier detection expert, scanning your data for those unusual suspects and flagging them for further investigation. It's like having a bloodhound with a nose for data anomalies, sniffing out anything that doesn't quite smell right.

From Raw Data to Actionable Insights: Copilot's Detective Work

Copilot doesn't just stop at identifying patterns and outliers. Additionally, it may assist you in converting your unprocessed data into insights that will advance the growth of your business. It can:

- **Generate Summaries and Reports:** Distill complex data into easy-to-understand summaries and reports that can be shared with stakeholders.
- **Visualize Data:** Create charts, graphs, and other visualizations that make your data come to life.
- **Identify Correlations and Relationships:** Discover hidden connections between different variables in your data.
- **Predict Future Trends:** Use machine learning algorithms to forecast future outcomes based on historical data.

Real-World Examples: Copilot's Data Detective Success Stories

Don't just take our word for it. Copilot has already helped countless businesses and individuals harness the power of their data.

- **The E-commerce Retailer:** Optimized their pricing strategy and increased sales by analyzing customer purchase patterns with Copilot's help.
- **The Healthcare Provider:** Improved patient outcomes by identifying risk factors and predicting readmission rates with Copilot's data analysis capabilities.
- **The Financial Analyst:** Made smarter investment decisions by uncovering market trends and predicting stock prices with Copilot's insights.

Your Data Analysis Partner in Crime:

With Copilot as your data detective, you can unlock the full potential of your data and gain a deeper understanding of your business, your customers, and your world.

Pro Tips for Data Analysis with Copilot:

- **Ask the Right Questions:** Before you start analyzing your data, clearly define the questions you want to answer.

- **Clean Your Data:** Ensure your data is accurate, complete, and free of errors before you start analyzing it.
- **Experiment with Different Visualizations:** Copilot can create a variety of charts and graphs. Experiment with different visualizations to find the ones that best communicate your insights.
- **Share Your Findings:** Don't keep your insights to yourself. Share your findings with your team or stakeholders to drive action and make informed decisions.

With Copilot by your side, you'll be a data detective extraordinaire, uncovering hidden treasures in your data and using them to achieve your goals.

Chart Champion:

Copilot, Your Data Visualization Virtuoso (No Artistic Talent Required)

Tired of staring at endless rows and columns of numbers? Ready to transform your boring spreadsheets into eye-catching, informative visuals? Look no further than Copilot, your chart champion extraordinaire!

Forget fumbling with complex charting tools or hiring expensive designers. Copilot can whip up stunning charts and graphs with a simple prompt, turning your data into a visual feast that's both informative and engaging.

Data Visualization Virtuoso: Painting Pictures with Numbers

Copilot is about using data to create stories rather than simply crunching numbers. And what better way to tell a story than with a picture?

With Copilot, you can transform your raw data into a symphony of colors, shapes, and patterns that reveal hidden insights, highlight trends, and make complex information easy to digest. It's like having a graphic designer and a data scientist rolled into one, working tirelessly to bring your data to life.

From Bar Charts to Bubble Charts: A Visual Feast

Copilot's chart-making repertoire is vast and varied. It can create:

- **Bar Charts:** Perfect for comparing values across different categories.
- **Line Graphs:** Ideal for visualizing trends over time.
- **Pie Charts:** Great for showing proportions and percentages.
- **Scatter Plots:** Useful for identifying relationships between two variables.
- **Heatmaps:** A colorful way to display data density or distribution.
- **And many more!**

Customize Your Creations: A Personal Touch

But Copilot doesn't just create cookie-cutter charts; it allows you to customize every aspect of your visuals. Colours, characters, labels, and even the kind of chart that best fits your data are all customizable. It's like having your own personal art studio, where you can create data visualizations that reflect your unique style and brand.

Real-World Examples: Copilot's Charting Triumphs

Don't just take our word for it. Copilot has already helped countless individuals and organizations turn their data into compelling visuals.

- **The Marketing Manager:** Created a visually stunning report that clearly communicated the impact of their latest campaign.
- **The Educator:** Engaged students and improved learning outcomes by using Copilot to create interactive charts and graphs.
- **The Data Analyst:** Uncovered hidden insights in their data by visualizing it in new and unexpected ways.

The Data Visualization Revolution: From Numbers to Narratives

With Copilot as your chart champion, you can revolutionize the way you present your data. It's time to embrace the potential of visual storytelling and throw out those dull spreadsheets.

Pro Tips for Data Visualization with Copilot:

- **Know Your Audience:** Consider who you're creating the visuals for and what information they need to know.
- **Keep It Simple:** Don't overload your charts with too much information. Pay attention to the main points you want to make.
- **Use Color Strategically:** Use colors to highlight important data points and create visual contrast.
- **Tell a Story:** Use your visuals to tell a compelling story about your data.
- **Get Creative:** Don't be afraid to experiment with different chart types and styles to find what works best for you.

With Copilot by your side, you'll be a data visualization virtuoso in no time. Now take out your mouse or virtual paintbrush and let's get to work painting some masterpieces!

Automation Ace:

Unleashing Your Inner Spreadsheet Superhero (No Cape Required, But It's Encouraged)

Tired of being chained to your spreadsheets, endlessly copying, pasting, and formatting data? Yearning to break free from the monotony of repetitive tasks and unleash your inner spreadsheet superhero? Look no further than Copilot, your automation ace in the hole!

Taskmaster: Your Digital Minion Army

Copilot isn't just about formulas and calculations; it's also a master of automation. With a few simple commands, you can unleash an army of digital minions to tackle those tedious tasks that drain your time and energy.

Think of it as having your own personal task force, tirelessly working in the background to:

- **Conquer Data Entry:** Let Copilot handle the drudgery of data entry, freeing you from mind-numbing copy-pasting.
- **Generate Reports on Autopilot:** Say goodbye to manually compiling data and formatting reports. Copilot can create customized reports with a few clicks, saving you hours of work.
- **Automate Repetitive Tasks:** Identify those mind-numbing tasks that you do over and over again, and let Copilot automate them for you.

Power Up Your Productivity:

Copilot's automation capabilities aren't just about saving time; they're about empowering you to be more productive and focus on the work that truly matters. With Copilot handling the mundane tasks, you can dedicate your energy to analyzing data, making strategic decisions, and driving your business forward.

Real-World Examples: Copilot's Automation Triumphs

Don't just take our word for it. Copilot has already helped countless Excel users automate their workflows and achieve new levels of productivity.

- **The Accountant:** Automated their monthly financial reporting process, saving them days of work and reducing the risk of errors.
- **The Marketing Manager:** Created a dynamic dashboard that automatically updates with the latest campaign data, providing real-time insights into performance.
- **The HR Professional:** Streamlined their employee onboarding process by automating data entry and generating personalized welcome emails.

Beyond the Basics: Power User Automation

Copilot's automation capabilities go far beyond the basics. With a little creativity and ingenuity, you can use it to automate complex workflows, create custom dashboards, and even build your own mini-applications within Excel.

Pro Tips for Automating with Copilot:

- **Start Small:** Begin by automating simple, repetitive tasks that you do frequently.
- **Think Big:** Once you've mastered the basics, start exploring more complex automation scenarios.

- **Use Copilot's Suggestions:** Copilot can often suggest ways to automate tasks that you might not have thought of.
- **Get Creative:** There are no limits to what you can automate with Copilot. Let your imagination run wild!

With Copilot as your automation ace, you can transform your Excel experience from tedious to terrific. It's time to ditch the drudgery, embrace the power of automation, and become the spreadsheet superhero you were born to be!

Custom Functions:

Brewing Your Own Excel Magic Potions (No Eye of Newt Required!)

Alright, spreadsheet sorcerers, prepare to level up your Excel alchemy! We've already seen how Copilot can conjure up formulas like a seasoned wizard. But now, get ready to brew your own custom functions – personalized spells that cater to your unique spreadsheet needs. Think of it as crafting your own secret sauce, a blend of Excel magic that'll make your spreadsheets sizzle with efficiency.

Why Custom Functions? Because Your Spreadsheets Are Special Snowflakes

Let's be honest: not every spreadsheet is created equal. You might be tracking sales data, analyzing marketing campaigns, or managing your fantasy football league. Copilot's built-in formulas are great, but they might not always cater to your specific needs. That's where custom functions come in, allowing you to create formulas tailored to your unique data and workflows.

With custom functions, you can:

- **Simplify Complex Calculations:** Break down complex formulas into smaller, more manageable chunks that are easier to understand and reuse.
- **Automate Repetitive Tasks:** Create functions that perform common tasks automatically, saving you time and effort.
- **Add a Personal Touch:** Inject your own personality and style into your spreadsheets with custom functions that reflect your unique approach.

Crafting Your Custom Function Concoctions: A Recipe for Success

Ready to start brewing your own Excel magic potions? Here's a simple recipe:

1. **Identify a Need:** Start by identifying a task or calculation that you perform frequently in Excel. This could be anything from cleaning up data to calculating specific metrics.
2. **Write Your Spell (Code):** Craft a VBA (Visual Basic for Applications) script that performs the desired task.

Don't worry if you're not a VBA expert – Copilot can help you write the code.

3. **Name Your Potion:** Give your custom function a clear, concise name that describes its purpose.
4. **Share Your Magic:** Once you've created your custom function, you can share it with your colleagues or the wider Excel community. Who knows, you might just become the next Excel Merlin!

Real-World Examples: Custom Function Enchantments

Need some inspiration? Here are a few examples of how custom functions have transformed the lives of Excel users:

- **The Data Analyst:** Created a custom function to calculate customer lifetime value, streamlining their analysis and providing valuable insights.
- **The Financial Planner:** Built a custom function to automate their portfolio rebalancing process, saving them hours of work and ensuring optimal asset allocation.
- **The Project Manager:** Developed a custom function to track project progress and identify potential bottlenecks, helping them keep their projects on track.

The Future of Excel: Your Personalized Spellbook

With Copilot as your guide, you can create a personalized spellbook of custom functions that empower you to do more with your data, automate your workflows, and unlock the full potential of Excel. So, grab your cauldron (or your keyboard) and start brewing some Excel magic!

Beyond Excel:

Data Storytelling: Turning Your Spreadsheets into Blockbusters (Popcorn Optional)

Alright, data nerds, prepare to transform those dry spreadsheets into Hollywood-worthy blockbusters! With Copilot as your storytelling sidekick, you'll be weaving captivating narratives, crafting compelling presentations, and captivating your audience with data-driven tales that are anything but boring.

Data Storytelling:

It's Not Just Numbers, It's a Narrative

Let's be honest: data can be a snoozefest. Endless rows and columns of numbers rarely inspire excitement or action. But with Copilot's data storytelling prowess, you can transform those numbers into a compelling narrative that grabs attention, sparks curiosity, and drives meaningful change.

Think of it as turning your spreadsheets into a thrilling movie, complete with heroes, villains, conflict, and resolution. With Copilot, you can weave together data points, insights, and anecdotes to create a story that resonates with your audience and leaves a lasting impact.

From Data Dumps to Compelling Presentations

Presentations are the bane of many professionals' existence. But with Copilot by your side, you can transform your data dumps into presentations that are not only informative but also engaging and persuasive.

Copilot can help you:

- **Craft a Compelling Storyline:** Develop a narrative arc that captures your audience's attention and keeps them engaged from start to finish.
- **Visualize Your Data:** Transform numbers into eye-catching charts, graphs, and infographics that make your data come to life.
- **Humanize Your Message:** Add anecdotes, personal experiences, and real-world examples to make your data relatable and memorable.

Real-World Examples: Copilot's Storytelling Success Stories

Don't just take our word for it. Copilot has already helped countless individuals and organizations turn their data into compelling stories.

- **The Nonprofit Director:** Secured funding for a critical project by using Copilot to create a presentation that moved donors to action.

- **The Marketing Manager:** Increased website traffic and conversions by using Copilot to craft data-driven blog posts and social media content.
- **The Scientist:** Communicated their research findings to a wider audience by using Copilot to create a compelling TED Talk.

Your Data Storytelling Dream Team:

With Copilot as your storytelling partner, you can unlock the full potential of your data and communicate your message with clarity, impact, and even a little bit of flair. It's time to ditch the boring presentations and embrace the power of data storytelling.

Pro Tips for Data Storytelling with Copilot:

- **Know Your Audience:** Tailor your story to your specific audience, considering their interests, knowledge level, and goals.
- **Focus on the "Why":** Don't just present the data; explain why it matters and what actions should be taken based on your findings.
- **Use Visuals Strategically:** Choose visuals that enhance your narrative and make your data easy to understand.
- **Practice Your Delivery:** Even the best story can fall flat if it's poorly delivered. Practice your presentation or

speech to ensure you deliver your message with confidence and impact.

With Copilot by your side, you'll be a data storytelling superstar, captivating your audience and driving meaningful change with your data-driven narratives. So, grab your popcorn (optional) and let's get this show on the road!

Integration with Power BI:

When Copilot Meets Power BI, It's Like Peanut Butter and Jelly (But for Data Nerds)

Alright, data wizards and dashboard aficionados, prepare to witness the ultimate power couple of the data world: Copilot and Power BI! When these two titans join forces, it's like peanut butter and jelly, cookies and milk, Batman and Robin – you get the idea. The result is a data analysis dream team that's greater than the sum of its parts.

Data Duet

Copilot's natural language processing prowess combined with Power BI's data visualization capabilities create a match made in (data) heaven. It's like having a data analyst and a graphic designer working side-by-side, seamlessly translating complex data into stunning visuals and actionable insights.

But this dynamic duo doesn't just look good together; they also work incredibly well together. Copilot is the ideal partner for Power BI because of its comprehension and responsiveness to natural language questions. This feature enables you to explore your data, derive insights, and produce reports with previously unheard-of simplicity.

Unleashing Copilot's Power in Power BI:

With Copilot integrated into Power BI, you can:

- **Ask Questions in Plain English:** No more wrestling with complex queries or DAX formulas. Simply ask Copilot questions like "What were our top-selling products last quarter?" or "Show me a trendline of our sales over the past year," and watch as it generates the answers and visuals in seconds.
- **Explore Your Data Like Never Before:** Copilot can help you discover hidden patterns, correlations, and outliers in your data, revealing insights you might have missed otherwise.
- **Create Custom Reports with Ease:** Generate comprehensive reports with a few clicks, complete with charts, graphs, and summaries tailored to your specific needs.
- **Collaborate and Share Insights:** Because of Power BI's collaboration capabilities, sharing your results with stakeholders and colleagues is simple and straightforward.

Real-World Examples: Copilot and Power BI Power Couples

Don't just take our word for it. Many companies have already benefited from using Copilot and Power BI to make data-driven choices that are more informed.

- **The Sales Team:** Identified their most profitable customer segments and tailored their sales strategies accordingly.
- **The Marketing Team:** Optimized their campaigns by analyzing customer engagement data and identifying high-performing channels.
- **The Executive Team:** Made strategic decisions based on real-time data insights, leading to increased revenue and profitability.

Beyond the Basics: Supercharging Your Data Analysis

Copilot's integration with Power BI is still in its early stages, but the possibilities are endless. As AI technology continues to evolve, we can expect to see even more powerful and intuitive ways to analyze and visualize data.

Pro Tips for Using Copilot in Power BI:

- **Be Clear and Concise:** When asking Copilot questions, be as specific as possible about what you want to know.
- **Experiment with Different Prompts:** Copilot can understand a wide range of natural language queries. Experiment with different phrasing to see what works best for you.

- **Give Feedback:** Help Copilot learn and improve by providing feedback on its responses and suggestions.

With Copilot and Power BI working together, you can unleash the full potential of your data and make smarter, faster, and more informed decisions. It's like having a team of data analysts and designers at your fingertips, ready to help you conquer the world of data!

CHAPTER NINE

Copilot for Presentations: Creating Engaging Slides

Slide Show Superstar: Ditch the Boring Decks and Unleash Your Inner Design Diva (No Bedazzler Required!)

Alright, presentation pros and PowerPoint ponderers, it's time to ditch those yawn-inducing slide decks and embrace a new era of visual storytelling! With Copilot as your design dynamo, you'll be crafting presentations that are so stunning, your audience might just forget they're in a meeting. Think Steve Jobs unveiling the first iPhone, but with less black turtleneck and more AI-powered awesomeness.

Design Dynamo: Your Personal PowerPoint Picasso

Forget those bland, corporate templates and clip art that screams "1995." Copilot is your personal design guru, ready to transform your slides into works of art that will leave your audience mesmerized.

Need help choosing a color scheme that pops? Copilot can suggest palettes that are both eye-catching and professional. Want to create a layout that's both visually appealing and easy to follow? Copilot can whip up a variety of options in seconds. It's like having a graphic designer on speed dial, minus the hefty hourly rate.

Beyond Pretty Pictures: Designing for Impact

But Copilot's design skills go beyond just making your slides look pretty. It can also help you communicate your message more effectively. It can suggest visual metaphors, infographics, and data visualizations that bring your ideas to life. It's like having a storytelling coach who knows how to use visuals to captivate your audience and drive your message home.

Template Transformer: From Bland to Brand

Don't settle for cookie-cutter templates that look like everyone else's. Copilot can help you transform those generic designs into something truly unique and reflective of your brand.

It can suggest fonts, colors, and graphics that align with your company's visual identity. It can even create custom templates that you can reuse for future presentations. It's like having a branding expert who understands the importance of consistency and visual appeal.

Real-World Examples: Copilot's Design Triumphs

Don't just take our word for it. Copilot has already helped countless individuals and organizations elevate their presentations from boring to brilliant.

- **The Startup Founder:** Secured funding from investors with a visually stunning pitch deck that showcased their product's potential.

- **The Marketing Team:** Generated buzz and excitement around a new product launch with a series of eye-catching social media posts and infographics.
- **The Educator:** Boosted student engagement and improved learning outcomes with interactive and visually appealing presentations.

Unleash Your Inner Design Diva (or Dude):

With Copilot as your design dynamo, you can unlock your creative potential and create presentations that are not only informative but also visually stunning and memorable. So, ditch the boring templates, embrace the power of AI, and become the presentation rockstar you were born to be!

Pro Tips for Designing with Copilot:

- **Start with a Clear Message:** Before you start designing, make sure you have a clear understanding of your message and your audience.
- **Use High-Quality Images:** Select visually attractive, high-resolution, and relevant photos.
- **Keep It Simple:** Don't overload your slides with too much text or too many visuals. Focus on the key points you want to convey.
- **Get Feedback:** Ask colleagues or friends for feedback on your designs before you present them to a larger audience.

With Copilot by your side, you'll be a design dynamo in no time. So, grab your virtual paintbrush and let's start creating some PowerPoint masterpieces!

Content Creator Extraordinaire:

From Blank Slides to Brilliant Ideas (No Caffeine Overdose Required!)

Alright, presentation pros, let's face it: staring at a blank slide is about as inspiring as watching a test pattern on an old TV. But fear not, because Copilot is your content creation sidekick, ready to fill those empty spaces with brilliance (and maybe a few well-placed memes).

The Idea Generator: From Brain Freeze to Brainstorm Blitz

Copilot isn't just a pretty face (or, well, a sleek interface). It's also a brainstorming powerhouse, ready to generate ideas faster than you can say "elevator pitch."

Need a catchy opening line? Copilot can suggest a few that'll hook your audience from the get-go. Stumped on how to summarize complex data? Let Copilot transform those numbers into a compelling story that even your grandma could understand. From witty anecdotes to thought-provoking questions, Copilot is your brainstorming buddy, always ready to spark your creativity.

Bullet Point Bonanza: Turning Walls of Text into Digestible Nuggets

Let's be honest: nobody wants to read a slide that looks like a page from a Tolstoy novel. Copilot can help you transform your walls of text into concise, easy-to-digest bullet points that convey your message with maximum impact.

Just feed Copilot your raw content, and it'll magically condense it into a series of bullet points that are both informative and visually appealing. It's like having a personal editor who's also a master of brevity.

Talking Point Wizard: Crafting Memorable Sound Bites

Want to leave your audience with a lasting impression? Copilot can help you craft memorable talking points that will stick in their minds long after your presentation is over.

Whether you need a pithy one-liner, a thought-provoking question, or a powerful call to action, Copilot can help you find the right words to resonate with your audience and leave them wanting more.

Real-World Examples: Copilot's Content Creation Prowess

Don't just take our word for it. Copilot has already helped countless presenters create content that informs, inspires, and entertains.

- **The Keynote Speaker:** Delivered a standing-ovation-worthy presentation with Copilot's help, crafting a narrative that captivated the audience and drove home their message.
- **The Sales Professional:** Closed a major deal after using Copilot to create a persuasive sales deck that highlighted the product's key benefits in a concise and compelling way.
- **The Teacher:** Engaged students and improved learning outcomes by using Copilot to create interactive and visually appealing presentations.

Your Presentation Partner in Crime:

With Copilot as your content creation companion, you can transform your presentations from boring to brilliant. It's time to ditch the generic templates, embrace the power of AI, and become the presentation rockstar you were born to be!

Pro Tips for Content Creation with Copilot:

- **Start with a Clear Message:** Before you start creating content, make sure you have a clear understanding of your message and your audience.
- **Use Keywords and Phrases:** Provide Copilot with relevant keywords and phrases to guide its suggestions.
- **Experiment with Different Prompts:** Try different prompts to see what kind of content Copilot generates.

- **Don't Be Afraid to Edit:** Copilot's suggestions are a starting point, not a finished product. Feel free to edit and refine them to fit your voice and style.

With Copilot by your side, you'll never have to face a blank slide again. Let your creativity flow, and let Copilot be your muse for content that clicks, converts, and keeps your audience engaged.

Presentation Pro:

Your Personal Presentation Coach (Minus the Whistle and Stopwatch)

Alright, presentation pros, it's time to take your slide decks from "meh" to "mesmerizing"! While Copilot can help you create stunning visuals and compelling content, it's not just about the slides themselves. It's about *how* you deliver your message. That's where Copilot's rehearsal, feedback, and Q&A management features come in. Think of it as your personal presentation coach, minus the whistle and stopwatch.

Rehearsal Room: Practice Makes Perfect (or at Least Less Painful)

Let's be honest: most of us dread practicing presentations. But with Copilot as your rehearsal buddy, practice becomes less painful and more productive. Copilot can:

- **Time Your Presentation:** Make sure you're not going over time by tracking your progress and alerting you if you're running long.
- **Identify Filler Words:** Catch those pesky "ums" and "ahs" that can undermine your credibility.
- **Analyze Your Pacing:** Ensure you're not speaking too quickly or too slowly by analyzing your speaking rate.
- **Suggest Improvements:** Offer tips on your body language, vocal variety, and overall delivery.

Feedback Loop: Getting Constructive Criticism (Without the Tears)

Ever wished you had a personal coach to give you feedback on your presentation skills? Well, Copilot can be your virtual mentor, providing constructive criticism that's both helpful and encouraging.

You can record your practice sessions and let Copilot analyze your delivery. It can identify areas where you can improve, such as:

- **Eye Contact:** Are you engaging your audience with your gaze, or are you staring at your notes?
- **Body Language:** Are you using gestures and movement to enhance your message, or are you standing like a statue?

- **Vocal Variety:** Is your voice monotone, or are you using inflection and emphasis to keep your audience engaged?

Q&A Champion: Handling Questions with Confidence

Q&A sessions can be a nerve-wracking experience, but with Copilot by your side, you can handle any question that comes your way. Copilot can:

Anticipate Questions: Copilot may provide suggestions for possible questions your audience might have based on the information in your presentation.

- **Provide Relevant Information:** If you get stumped by a question, Copilot can quickly search your presentation and other resources to find the information you need.
- **Suggest Follow-Up Questions:** Help you keep the conversation going by suggesting follow-up questions or topics.

The Presentation Transformation: From Nervous Novice to Confident Pro

With Copilot as your presentation coach, you can transform your presentation skills and deliver talks that are not only informative but also engaging, persuasive, and memorable.

So, the next time you have to give a presentation, don't stress. Just fire up Copilot, let it work its magic, and get ready to wow your audience!

Pro Tips for Rehearsing with Copilot:

- **Practice in a Realistic Setting:** If possible, practice in the same room or environment where you'll be giving your presentation.
- **Record Yourself:** Record your practice sessions so you can review them later and identify areas for improvement.
- **Get Feedback from Others:** Ask friends, colleagues, or family members to watch your practice sessions and give you feedback.
- **Use Copilot's Suggestions:** Don't be afraid to implement Copilot's suggestions and feedback to improve your delivery.

With Copilot by your side, you'll be a presentation pro in no time. So, go forth and conquer those speaking engagements!

Beyond Slides:

Multimedia Maven: Transforming Your Presentations from Snoozefest to Sensations (No Film Degree Required)

Alright, presentation pros, it's time to ditch the boring bullet points and static images! You must improve your multimedia skills if you want to really engage your audience and make an impact. Thankfully, Copilot is here to transform you into a multimedia maven, even if you've never touched a video editing software in your life.

The Multimedia Mixer: Blending Visuals, Audio, and More

Copilot isn't just a wordsmith; it's also a multimedia maestro. It can help you seamlessly integrate images, videos, and audio into your presentations, creating a multi-sensory experience that will keep your audience on the edge of their seats (or at least, prevent them from dozing off).

Think of Copilot as your personal DJ, mixing and matching different media elements to create a presentation that's both informative and entertaining. With Copilot, you can:

- **Find the Perfect Image:** Search for high-quality images that complement your content and capture your audience's attention.
- **Embed Videos:** Add video clips that illustrate your points, tell a story, or simply add a touch of humor.

- **Incorporate Audio:** Use sound effects, background music, or even your own voiceover narration to improve your presentation.

Beyond PowerPoint: A World of Multimedia Possibilities

Copilot's multimedia capabilities extend beyond PowerPoint. It can also help you create engaging content for other platforms, such as:

- **Social Media:** Craft eye-catching videos and GIFs that will go viral.
- **Websites and Blogs:** Embed videos and audio to make your content more interactive and engaging.
- **Online Courses:** Create multimedia-rich learning experiences that captivate your students.

Real-World Examples: Copilot's Multimedia Magic

Don't just take our word for it. Copilot has already helped countless creators elevate their multimedia game.

- **The YouTuber:** Increased their views and subscribers by using Copilot to generate eye-catching thumbnails and engaging video scripts.
- **The Marketing Team:** Boosted their social media engagement with Copilot-created GIFs and videos that went viral.
- **The Teacher:** Created interactive lessons that captivated students and improved learning outcomes by

incorporating multimedia elements suggested by Copilot.

Pro Tips for Mastering Multimedia with Copilot:

- **Choose Wisely:** Not every presentation needs to be a multimedia extravaganza. Use multimedia strategically to enhance your message, not overwhelm your audience.
- **Keep It Relevant:** Ensure that the multimedia components you use are pertinent to your subject and enhance your presentation.
- **Quality Matters:** Employ top-notch pictures, audio, and video to give your content a polished and professional appearance.
- **Test Your Tech:** Before you present, make sure your multimedia elements are working properly and that you have the necessary equipment.

Unleash Your Inner Spielberg:

With Copilot as your multimedia maven, you can transform your presentations from boring to brilliant. So, grab your virtual camera and let's start creating some cinematic masterpieces!

Interactive Elements:

Turning Your Presentations into a Game Show (Minus the Cheesy Prizes, But Hey, Who Doesn't Love a Little Audience Participation?)

Alright, presentation pros, are you ready to take audience engagement to the next level? Forget death by PowerPoint and say hello to presentations that are so interactive, your audience will be begging for more. With Copilot as your interactive guru, you'll be transforming your slides into a game show, a quiz bowl, or even a choose-your-own-adventure story.

Gamification Galore: Turning Learning into Play

Let's be honest: sitting through a long presentation can be a real snoozefest. But with Copilot's interactive features, you can inject some fun and excitement into your presentations, turning them into a game show that your audience will actually enjoy.

Copilot can help you create:

- **Polls:** Ask your audience for immediate comments to find out how well they comprehend your subject.
- **Quizzes:** Test your audience's knowledge and make learning fun.
- **Interactive Games:** Break the ice and get your audience laughing and participating.

- **Choose-Your-Own-Adventure Stories:** Create branching narratives that allow your audience to choose their own path through your presentation.

Beyond Fun and Games: Driving Engagement and Retention

But interactive elements aren't just about fun and games; they're also a powerful tool for driving engagement and retention. When your audience is actively participating in your presentation, they're more likely to pay attention, remember your message, and take action.

Copilot can help you create interactive elements that:

- **Spark Curiosity:** Encourage your audience to ask questions and explore your topic in more depth.
- **Promote Collaboration:** Facilitate discussions and brainstorming sessions that lead to new ideas and solutions.
- **Reinforce Learning:** Help your audience retain information by actively applying it in a fun and engaging way.

Real-World Examples: Copilot's Interactive Innovations

Don't just take our word for it. Copilot has already helped countless presenters transform their presentations into interactive experiences.

- **The Teacher:** Boosted student engagement and improved test scores by incorporating quizzes and games into their lessons.
- **The Marketing Manager:** Increased audience participation and generated valuable leads by using polls and surveys in their presentations.
- **The Conference Speaker:** Created a buzzworthy keynote that got people talking and sharing on social media, thanks to interactive elements like a live Twitter feed and a Q&A session.

Pro Tips for Interactive Presentations with Copilot:

- **Keep It Simple:** Don't overload your presentation with too many interactive elements. Choose a few that align with your goals and audience.
- **Test It Out:** Before you present, test your interactive elements to make sure they're working properly.
- **Be Prepared for Anything:** Have a backup plan in case your technology fails or your audience doesn't participate as expected.
- **Most Importantly: Have Fun!** Interactive presentations are meant to be enjoyable for both you and your audience. So, relax, have fun, and let Copilot be your guide.

The Interactive Advantage:

With Copilot as your interactive guru, you can transform your presentations from boring lectures into engaging experiences that will leave a lasting impression on your audience. So, ditch the clicker, embrace the power of AI, and get ready to become the presentation pro you were born to be!

The Presenter's Partner:

Your Anti-Anxiety Amulet for Presentation Panic (No Xanax Required!)

Alright, my fellow stage fright sufferers, raise your hand if you've ever experienced sweaty palms, racing heartbeats, and a sudden urge to flee the scene moments before a presentation. (Don't worry, we won't judge – we've all been there.)

But fear not, because Copilot is here to be your virtual hype-person, cheerleader, and confidence coach. Think of it as your anti-anxiety amulet, banishing those pre-presentation jitters and empowering you to deliver your message with poise, charisma, and maybe even a little bit of swagger.

Conquering Stage Fright: Your Inner Superhero Awaits

Let's be real: stage fright is a beast. It can turn even the most eloquent speaker into a bumbling mess. But here's the good news: you're not alone. Many successful presenters have battled stage fright, and with Copilot as your ally, you can too.

Copilot can't magically erase your nerves, but it can help you manage them. It can provide:

- **Virtual Reassurance:** Copilot can offer words of encouragement and support, reminding you of your strengths and past successes.
- **Breathing Exercises:** Calm your nerves with guided breathing exercises that help you relax and focus.
- **Positive Affirmations:** Reprogram your mind with positive self-talk that boosts your confidence.
- **Visualization Techniques:** Imagine yourself delivering a successful presentation, feeling confident and in control.

Delivery Dynamo: Polishing Your Performance

But Copilot isn't just about calming your nerves; it's also about helping you deliver your presentation with poise and impact. It can:

- **Analyze Your Body Language:** Ensure you're making eye contact, using appropriate gestures, and projecting confidence.
- **Fine-Tune Your Pacing:** Help you find the right balance between speaking too quickly and too slowly.
- **Improve Your Vocal Variety:** Suggest ways to use inflection, tone, and volume to keep your audience engaged.

The Q&A Masterclass: Handling Curveballs Like a Pro

The Q&A portion of a presentation can be a minefield, but with Copilot in your corner, you can handle any question that comes your way. Copilot can:

- **Anticipate Questions:** Based on the content of your presentation, Copilot can suggest potential questions your audience might ask.
- **Provide Relevant Information:** If you get stumped, Copilot can quickly search your presentation and other resources to find the information you need.
- **Offer Suggested Responses:** Help you craft clear, concise, and compelling answers to even the most challenging questions.

Real-World Examples: Copilot's Confidence-Boosting Success Stories

Don't just take our word for it. Copilot has already helped countless individuals overcome their stage fright and deliver presentations that left a lasting impact.

- **The Shy Introvert:** Delivered a keynote address to a packed auditorium, thanks to Copilot's calming techniques and positive affirmations.
- **The Nervous Job Candidate:** Aced their interview presentation, impressing the hiring manager with their confident delivery and well-prepared answers.
- **The Public Speaking Phobic:** Discovered a newfound love for public speaking after using Copilot to

build their confidence and polish their presentation skills.

From Stage Fright to Stage Right:

With Copilot as your presentation partner, you can conquer your fears, embrace your inner superhero, and deliver presentations that are not only informative but also inspiring and impactful. So, take a deep breath, step into the spotlight, and let Copilot be your guide on this journey to presentation mastery.

Audience Engager:

Turning Spectators into Superfans (No Pom-Poms or Chants Required, But They're Welcome)

Alright, presentation pros, are you ready to transform your audience from passive spectators into raving superfans? Forget those boring lectures and death-by-PowerPoint presentations. With Copilot as your Audience Engager, you'll be creating presentations that are so captivating, your audience will be hanging on your every word (and maybe even tweeting about it).

The Engagement Enhancer: Turning Monologues into Conversations

Let's be honest: nobody likes to be talked *at* for hours on end. Copilot can help you transform your presentations from one-sided monologues into dynamic conversations that involve your audience and keep them on the edge of their seats.

Copilot can help you:

- **Ask Thought-Provoking Questions:** Spark discussions and get your audience thinking critically about your topic.
- **Incorporate Polls and Surveys:** Gather instant feedback and gauge your audience's opinions and understanding.
- **Use Humor and Storytelling:** Keep your audience entertained and engaged with anecdotes, jokes, and personal stories.
- **Create Interactive Activities:** Get your audience involved with quizzes, games, or other hands-on activities.

Beyond Engagement: Building Relationships That Last

But audience engagement isn't just about keeping people awake during your presentation; it's about building lasting relationships with your audience. Copilot can help you connect with your audience on a deeper level, leaving a lasting impression and fostering a sense of community.

Copilot can help you:

- **Personalize Your Message:** Tailor your content and delivery to your specific audience, taking into account their interests, needs, and pain points.
- **Show Your Authenticity:** Share your passion for your topic and let your personality shine through.

- **Be Vulnerable:** Don't be afraid to share personal stories or anecdotes that make you relatable and human.
- **Follow Up:** After your presentation, connect with your audience on social media or through email to continue the conversation.

Real-World Examples: Copilot's Engagement Enchantments

Don't just take our word for it. Copilot has already helped countless presenters connect with their audiences and create memorable experiences.

- **The Keynote Speaker:** Received rave reviews for their engaging and interactive presentation, which sparked lively discussions and generated valuable insights.
- **The Workshop Facilitator:** Created a collaborative and productive learning environment by using Copilot to facilitate group activities and discussions.
- **The Sales Professional:** Built rapport with potential clients by using Copilot to personalize their presentations and tailor their message to each individual.

Your Audience Engagement Arsenal:

With Copilot as your secret weapon, you can transform your presentations from forgettable lectures into unforgettable experiences. So, let's ditch the boring bullet points, embrace the power of interaction, and turn your audience into raving superfans!

SECTION C

Advanced Copilot Techniques: Taking Your Skills to the Next Level

CHAPTER TEN

Customization: *Tailoring Copilot to Your Needs*

Copilot, Your Way: *Molding Your AI Sidekick into the Perfect Companion (No Frankensteinian Experiments Required, But We Won't Judge)*

Alright, personalization pros and customization connoisseurs, get ready to turn Copilot into your ideal digital sidekick! We're not talking about a simple name change or a new profile picture; we're talking about molding Copilot's personality, behavior, and capabilities to perfectly match your workflow and preferences. Think of it as customizing your own virtual assistant, but without the creepy feeling of being constantly monitored. (We promise, Copilot won't judge your questionable taste in music.)

The Personalization Playground:

Where Your AI Dreams Come True

Copilot isn't just a one-size-fits-all AI; it's a customizable canvas for your digital dreams. Want Copilot to sound like a wise old sage, a sassy comedian, or even your favorite celebrity? No problem! Want it to write in a formal tone for work emails but a casual tone for social media posts? You got it!

Copilot's personalization playground is where you get to play Dr. Frankenstein (in a good way), sculpting your AI assistant into the perfect companion for your unique needs and preferences.

Voice & Tone:

From Shakespearean Scholar to Stand-Up Comic (Copilot's Got Range!)

Tired of your AI assistant sounding like a monotonous robot or a stuffy professor? Get ready to give Copilot a personality makeover! With just a few tweaks, you can transform your digital sidekick into a linguistic chameleon, capable of adapting its voice and tone to match your own unique style.

The Voiceover Vault: Choose Your Character

Copilot comes with a pre-loaded cast of characters, each with its own distinct voice and personality. Want a wise old sage to guide you through your day? There's a voice for that. Need a peppy cheerleader to pump you up? Copilot's got you covered. Craving a sarcastic sidekick to make you chuckle? Look no further.

But the fun doesn't stop there. If you're feeling adventurous, you can even create your own custom voice by recording your own samples or using text-to-speech technology. Imagine

Copilot sounding like Morgan Freeman, Oprah Winfrey, or even your eccentric Uncle Bob. The possibilities are endless!

Tone It Up (or Down): Setting the Mood

Once you've chosen your voice, it's time to set the tone. Copilot can adapt its communication style to match your needs, whether you're writing a formal business email, a casual blog post, or a hilarious social media caption.

You can adjust Copilot's tone by using keywords and phrases in your prompts. For example, try "write a professional email" or "draft a playful social media post." You can even get specific with requests like "write a persuasive sales pitch" or "summarize this article in a witty way."

Real-World Examples: Copilot's Voice and Tone Makeovers

Still not convinced? Here are a few examples of how Copilot can transform its voice and tone to fit different scenarios:

- Formal: "Greetings, esteemed colleague. I am writing to inquire about the progress of the aforementioned project."
- Casual: "Hey there! Just checking in to see how things are going. How's the project coming along?"
- Humorous: "Well, well, well, look who's finally decided to grace us with their presence. How's it hangin', project master?"

The Power of Personalization: A Voice That's Uniquely Yours

By customizing Copilot's voice and tone, you're not just creating a more pleasant user experience; you're forging a deeper connection with your AI assistant. A Copilot that speaks in a way that resonates with you is more likely to become an indispensable part of your workflow, a trusted confidant, and even a source of amusement.

So, don't be afraid to experiment and find the perfect voice and tone for your Copilot. Whether you want a serious scholar, a playful companion, or something in between, the choice is yours. With Copilot, you can create an AI assistant that truly reflects your personality and style.

Pro Tips for Mastering Voice and Tone:

- **Provide Feedback:** The more you interact with Copilot, the better it gets at understanding your preferences. So, don't hesitate to give feedback on its responses and suggestions.
- **Experiment with Different Settings:** Copilot offers a variety of voice and tone options. Don't be afraid to try them all and see what works best for you.

- **Have Fun:** Personalizing Copilot should be a fun and creative process. So, let your imagination run wild and create a digital sidekick that's truly one of a kind!

Domain Expertise:

From Jack-of-All-Trades to Master of Your Domain (No PhD Required!)

Think of Copilot as a bright-eyed intern, eager to learn the ropes of your industry. With a little guidance, this AI whiz kid can quickly become a valuable asset, speaking your lingo, understanding your jargon, and even offering insights that you might have missed. It's like having a specialized consultant who's always on call, but without the hefty consulting fees.

The Learning Curve: From Novice to Expert in Record Time

Copilot's ability to learn and adapt is truly remarkable. By feeding it relevant information and examples, you can teach it the ins and outs of your specific domain. Think of it as giving Copilot a crash course in your industry, complete with vocabulary lessons, case studies, and even a few war stories.

The more you teach Copilot, the more valuable it becomes. It can:

- **Understand Your Jargon:** Decipher those cryptic acronyms and industry-specific terms that would leave outsiders scratching their heads.
- **Provide Relevant Suggestions:** Offer insights and solutions that are tailored to your specific challenges and goals.
- **Generate Industry-Specific Content:** Craft emails, reports, or presentations that sound like they were written by a seasoned professional in your field.

Real-World Examples: Copilot's Domain Expertise in Action

Don't just take our word for it. Copilot has already proven its value across a wide range of industries:

- **Healthcare:** Helping doctors and nurses summarize patient notes, draft medical reports, and even generate treatment plans.
- **Finance:** Assisting financial analysts with complex calculations, risk assessments, and investment strategies.
- **Marketing:** Crafting compelling ad copy, social media posts, and email campaigns that resonate with target audiences.

- **Legal:** Drafting contracts, summarizing legal documents, and conducting research on specific laws and regulations.
- **Education:** Creating lesson plans, grading assignments, and providing personalized feedback to students.

Your Domain Expertise Toolkit: Teaching Copilot the Ropes

Ready to transform Copilot into your industry insider? Here are a few tips:

- **Feed It the Right Data:** Provide Copilot with relevant documents, articles, and data sets from your industry.
- **Use Specific Prompts:** When asking Copilot for help, use industry-specific language and terminology.
- **Give Feedback:** Let Copilot know when its suggestions are on point and when they need improvement.

The Domain Expertise Advantage: A Competitive Edge

By investing time and effort into teaching Copilot about your domain, you're not just creating a more helpful AI assistant;

you're gaining a competitive edge. A Copilot that understands your industry inside and out can help you:

- **Work Smarter:** Automate repetitive tasks, streamline workflows, and free up your time for more strategic work.
- **Make Better Decisions:** Get access to relevant data and insights that can inform your decision-making process.
- **Stay Ahead of the Curve:** Stay up-to-date with the latest trends and developments in your industry.

The Future of Domain Expertise: Your AI Co-Pilot

As AI technology continues to advance, we can expect Copilot's domain expertise to become even more sophisticated. Imagine a future where Copilot is not just a tool but a true collaborator, working alongside you to solve complex problems, generate innovative ideas, and achieve your goals.

So, don't be afraid to invest in Copilot's education. The more you teach it, the more it can help you. With Copilot as your domain expert, the possibilities are endless.

Under the Hood:

Tweaking the Knobs and Dials of Your AI Sidekick (Safety Goggles Recommended, Just in Case)

Alright, tinkerers and tech aficionados, it's time to roll up our sleeves and get our hands dirty! We've explored Copilot's user-friendly interface, but now we're delving into the engine room, where you can fine-tune your AI assistant's behavior to match your exact preferences. Think of it as customizing a high-performance sports car: you can tweak the suspension, adjust the throttle response, and even add a few aftermarket modifications to make it truly your own.

Advanced Settings:

The Copilot Customization Cockpit

Just like a car's dashboard, Copilot's advanced settings menu is where you take control. It's a treasure trove of options and sliders that let you fine-tune everything from its vocabulary to its verbosity. Here are a few of the key settings you can tinker with:

- **Response Length:** Do you prefer short, snappy answers, or do you crave detailed, in-depth explanations? Adjust this slider to control the length of Copilot's responses.
- **Creativity Level:** Want Copilot to think outside the box and generate wild ideas? Or would you prefer it to

stick to the facts and play it safe? This setting lets you control Copilot's creative juices.

- **Tone:** We've already talked about how to adjust Copilot's tone through prompts, but you can also set a default tone here. Want Copilot to always be polite and professional? Or would you prefer a more casual, conversational tone?
- **Risk Tolerance:** How adventurous do you want Copilot to be? Do you want it to suggest bold, experimental ideas, or would you rather it stick to tried-and-true solutions?

Real-World Examples: Tweaking Copilot to Fit Your Needs

Here are a few examples of how you can use Copilot's advanced settings to customize your experience:

- **The Novelist:** Crank up the creativity level to get Copilot to help brainstorm plot twists and character arcs.
- **The Data Analyst:** Set the response length to "detailed" to get in-depth explanations of complex data analysis results.

- **The Social Media Manager:** Adjust the tone to "playful" to generate witty captions and social media posts.
- **The Developer:** Set the risk tolerance to "low" to ensure that Copilot's code suggestions are safe and reliable.

Pro Tips for Tweaking Your AI Sidekick:

- **Experiment:** Don't be afraid to experiment with different settings to see what works best for you.
- **Start Slowly:** If you're new to Copilot, start with the default settings and gradually adjust them as you become more familiar with its capabilities.
- **Read the Documentation:** Microsoft provides detailed documentation on Copilot's advanced settings. Take some time to read it and understand what each setting does.
- **Back It Up:** Before you make any major changes, back up your Copilot settings just in case you want to revert to them later.

The Customization Conundrum: Finding the Perfect Balance

Remember, customizing Copilot is all about finding the right balance for you. There's no one-size-fits-all solution, so experiment, have fun, and create an AI assistant that's perfectly tailored to your needs and preferences.

Plugins & Extensions:

Supercharging Your Copilot with Add-Ons (No, Not the Hairspray Kind)

Alright, fellow power users, are you ready to take your Copilot experience to ludicrous speed? While Copilot is already a multi-talented marvel, its capabilities can be further expanded with the help of plugins and extensions. Think of them as add-ons for your AI sidekick, like giving it a jetpack, a pair of X-ray vision goggles, or even a Swiss Army knife (but with more coding tools).

Copilot's App Store: A Candy Store for Productivity Geeks

Copilot's plugin and extension marketplace is like a candy store for productivity geeks. You'll find a treasure trove of add-ons designed to enhance your Copilot experience in various ways. Need to summarize lengthy documents in a flash? There's a plugin for that. Want to translate your code into different programming languages? Copilot's got you covered. Craving real-time stock market updates? Yep, there's a plugin for that too.

The beauty of plugins and extensions is that they allow you to customize Copilot to fit your specific needs and interests. Whether you're a writer, a developer, a marketer, or a data analyst, there's a plugin out there that can help you streamline your workflow and boost your productivity.

Supercharging Your Workflow: A Few Plugin Power-Ups

Here are a few examples of how plugins and extensions can supercharge your Copilot experience:

- **Document Summarizer:** Condense lengthy articles, reports, or emails into bite-sized summaries in seconds.
- **Code Translator:** Translate code between different programming languages with ease.
- **Data Visualization:** Transform your data into eye-catching charts and graphs.
- **Project Management:** Integrate with project management tools to track tasks, deadlines, and progress.
- **Language Learning:** Get real-time translations and grammar corrections in multiple languages.
- **And Many More!** The possibilities are endless, and new plugins and extensions are being added all the time.

Installing and Managing Plugins: It's Easier Than Assembling IKEA Furniture (Probably)

Installing and managing Copilot plugins is a breeze. Simply head to the Copilot marketplace, browse the available options, and click "Install." Copilot will handle the rest, seamlessly integrating the plugin into its interface.

You can also easily manage your installed plugins, enabling or disabling them as needed. It's like having a control panel for your AI assistant, allowing you to customize its capabilities on the fly.

The Future of Copilot: A Modular Marvel

With its growing library of plugins and extensions, Copilot is evolving into a modular marvel. You can pick and choose the features you need, creating a personalized AI assistant that's perfectly tailored to your workflow and preferences. It's like building your own custom robot, but without the soldering iron and wires.

Pro Tips for Plugin Power Users:

- **Explore the Marketplace:** Take some time to browse the Copilot marketplace and discover the wide range of available plugins and extensions.
- **Read Reviews:** Before installing a plugin, read the reviews to see what other users think of it.

- **Start with the Essentials:** Don't overload Copilot with too many plugins at once. Start with the ones that you think will be most useful for your work.
- **Experiment:** Don't be afraid to try out different plugins and see how they work for you. You might be surprised at what you discover.

With plugins and extensions, you can unlock Copilot's full potential and create a truly personalized AI experience. So, what are you waiting for? Head to the marketplace and start exploring!

API Access (for Developers):

Supercharging Your Copilot with Code-Fu (Black Belt in Coding Optional, But Encouraged)

Calling all code wranglers and digital architects! Are you ready to unlock the full potential of your AI sidekick and turn Copilot into a custom-built coding powerhouse? Then grab your keyboard (and maybe a Red Bull) because we're about to delve into the world of API access, where you can unleash Copilot's raw power and bend it to your will.

What's an API, Anyway? (And Why Should You Care?)

API stands for Application Programming Interface. Think of it as a set of tools and protocols that allow different software applications to talk to each other. It's like a universal translator for code, enabling different programs to share data, exchange commands, and work together seamlessly.

With Copilot's API, you can tap into its vast knowledge base, language processing capabilities, and code generation skills. You can then integrate Copilot into your own applications, creating custom workflows, automating tasks, and building tools that were previously unimaginable.

Unleashing the Beast: Copilot's API in Action

Here are just a few examples of how developers are using Copilot's API to supercharge their productivity:

- **Custom Code Generation:** Create tools that generate code snippets, templates, or even entire functions based on natural language descriptions.
- **Intelligent Automation:** Automate repetitive coding tasks, such as writing boilerplate code, refactoring, or generating documentation.
- **Enhanced IDE Integration:** Embed Copilot's capabilities directly into your favorite code editor, making it an even more powerful coding companion.
- **Natural Language Interfaces:** Build applications that allow users to interact with your code using natural language commands.

API Deep Dive: Getting Your Hands Dirty

Ready to get your hands dirty with Copilot's API? Here's what you need to know:

- **Documentation:** Start by diving into the official Copilot API documentation. It's your treasure map to all the available endpoints, parameters, and response formats.
- **Authentication:** You'll need to obtain an API key to access Copilot's services. This key acts like a password, ensuring that only authorized users can access the API.
- **Libraries and SDKs:** Microsoft provides libraries and SDKs (software development kits) for various programming languages, making it easier to integrate Copilot into your projects.
- **Experimentation:** The best way to learn is by doing. Start by experimenting with simple API calls, and then gradually build up to more complex integrations.

The Future of Copilot: A Playground for Developers

With its powerful API, Copilot is more than just an AI assistant; it's a platform for innovation. By opening up its capabilities to developers, Microsoft is creating a vibrant ecosystem of custom tools, applications, and integrations that are pushing the boundaries of what's possible with AI.

Pro Tips for API Adventurers:

- **Read the Docs:** Thoroughly read the Copilot API documentation before you start building. It's your best friend on this journey.
- **Start Small:** Begin with simple API calls to get a feel for how it works.
- **Ask for Help:** If you get stuck, don't hesitate to reach out to the Copilot community for support.
- **Share Your Creations:** Share your custom integrations with the world and inspire others to build amazing things with Copilot.

With Copilot's API, you have the power to create your own AI-powered tools and workflows. So, embrace your inner developer, unleash your creativity, and let's build the future of coding together!

Copilot's Secret Sauce:

Unraveling the AI Enigma (No Decoding Rings or Secret Handshakes Required!)

Alright, tech aficionados and AI enthusiasts, prepare to have your minds blown! We've seen Copilot in action, marveling at its ability to write emails, generate code, and even crack jokes.

But what exactly makes this AI assistant tick? What's the secret sauce behind its seemingly magical abilities?

The AI Enigma: Peering into the Black Box

Copilot's inner workings might seem like a mysterious black box, but we're about to shed some light on the technology that powers this AI marvel. Don't worry, we won't bore you with technical jargon. We'll keep it simple, fun, and informative, just like a good old-fashioned science fair project (minus the baking soda volcanoes).

At its core, Copilot is built on a type of artificial intelligence called a Large Language Model (LLM). This model is trained on a massive dataset of text and code, allowing it to understand the nuances of human language and generate responses that are both relevant and coherent.

The Learning Machine: Copilot's Journey of Knowledge

Think of Copilot as a sponge, soaking up information from a vast ocean of data. It's been fed a steady diet of books, articles, code repositories, and even social media posts. This massive amount of information allows Copilot to understand the intricacies of language, grammar, and syntax, as well as the patterns and conventions of different writing styles and coding practices.

But Copilot isn't just memorizing information; it's learning to reason, make inferences, and even generate creative content. It's like a student who's constantly learning and growing, becoming more knowledgeable and sophisticated with each new piece of information it encounters.

The Power of Prediction: Copilot's Crystal Ball

One of Copilot's most impressive abilities is its power of prediction. Based on the context of your request, it can anticipate your needs and generate suggestions that are not only relevant but also often surprisingly accurate.

It's like having a mind-reading assistant who knows what you want before you even ask. This predictive power is what allows Copilot to complete your sentences, suggest relevant code snippets, and even generate creative ideas on your behalf.

The Human Touch: A Collaboration Between Man and Machine

While Copilot's AI model is impressive, it's important to remember that it's not a replacement for human creativity and expertise. It's a tool, a collaborator, an extension of your own capabilities.

Together, AI and humans are capable of incredible feats. Copilot can handle the tedious tasks, freeing you up to focus on the big picture, the creative vision, the strategic thinking that only humans are capable of.

The Future of AI: A Glimpse into the Possibilities

Copilot is just the beginning. As AI technology continues to advance, we can expect to see even more sophisticated and powerful AI assistants that can not only help us with our work but also enhance our creativity, expand our knowledge, and even improve our well-being.

The future of AI is bright, and Copilot is leading the way. So, buckle up and get ready for an exciting journey into the world of artificial intelligence!

Training & Feedback:

Nurturing Your AI Padawan into a Jedi Master (Lightsaber Training Optional)

Alright, padawans of productivity, it's time to take your relationship with Copilot to the next level! Think of Copilot as a young Jedi apprentice, eager to learn and grow under your expert guidance. With a little patience, encouragement, and the occasional constructive criticism, you can mold Copilot into a powerful ally, a trusted advisor, and maybe even a bit of a comedian (if that's your thing).

Training Your AI Padawan: It's All About the Data

Like any good student, Copilot learns by example. The more you use it, the more data it gathers about your writing style, preferences, and areas of expertise. This data helps Copilot fine-tune its algorithms, improve its suggestions, and become a more valuable assistant over time.

Think of it like training a puppy. You wouldn't expect your furry friend to fetch the newspaper on the first try, right? It takes time, patience, and consistent reinforcement to teach new tricks. The same goes for Copilot. It becomes more intelligent the more you use it.

Here are a few ways to train your AI padawan:

- **Use It Regularly:** The more you use Copilot, the more data it has to work with. So, make it a habit to use it for all your writing, coding, and data analysis tasks.
- **Provide Diverse Input:** Don't just use Copilot for one type of task. Give it a variety of challenges, from writing emails to summarizing articles to generating code snippets.
- **Be Patient:** Copilot is still learning and growing. It might make mistakes or offer suggestions that aren't quite right. That's okay! Just give it time and feedback, and it will improve.

Feedback: Your Jedi Master Wisdom

Your feedback is essential for Copilot's growth and development. Think of yourself as Yoda, imparting your wisdom to a young Luke Skywalker. Your guidance will help Copilot become a more powerful and intuitive assistant.

Here's how to give feedback to Copilot:

- **Rate Its Suggestions:** Most Copilot interfaces have a thumbs-up/thumbs-down rating system. Use it to let Copilot know when its suggestions are helpful or not.
- **Provide Specific Feedback:** If Copilot makes a mistake or offers a suggestion that's off-base, explain why. The more specific your feedback, the more Copilot can learn from it.
- **Suggest Alternatives:** If you have a better way of phrasing something or a different solution to a problem, share it with Copilot.

The Training Payoff: A Jedi Master in the Making

By investing time and effort into training and providing feedback to Copilot, you're not just creating a more helpful AI assistant; you're shaping the future of AI. Your input will help Copilot become a more powerful, intuitive, and personalized tool that can truly enhance your work and creativity.

So, embrace your role as a Jedi master, and let's guide Copilot on its path to becoming the ultimate AI assistant!

Pro Tips for Training and Feedback:

- **Be Consistent:** Provide feedback regularly, not just when Copilot makes a mistake.
- **Be Positive:** Don't just focus on negative feedback. Let Copilot know when it does something well.
- **Be Patient:** It takes time for Copilot to learn and improve. Don't get discouraged if it doesn't always get it right the first time.

With your guidance, Copilot can become a powerful ally, helping you achieve your goals and unleash your full potential.

CHAPTER ELEVEN

Troubleshooting: *Overcoming Common Challenges*

Copilot's Quirks: *When Your AI Sidekick Goes Rogue (But in a Mostly Harmless Way)*

Alright, fellow Copilot adventurers, it's time for a reality check. While Copilot is undoubtedly a brilliant AI assistant, it's not perfect. Like any good sidekick, it has its quirks, its foibles, and its occasional moments of "What were you thinking?"

In this chapter, we'll delve into the fascinating world of Copilot's quirks, exploring why it sometimes gets things wrong, how to spot those missteps, and how to get back on track when things go awry. Think of it as a friendly PSA for navigating the sometimes unpredictable world of AI.

"Hallucinations" and Misinterpretations:

When Copilot's Imagination Runs Wild

One of Copilot's most intriguing (and occasionally frustrating) quirks is its tendency to "hallucinate" or misinterpret information. This is when Copilot generates responses that are factually incorrect, illogical, or simply nonsensical.

It's like asking Copilot for directions to the nearest coffee shop, and it tells you to take a left turn into a brick wall. It's a bit like that friend who always tells the most outlandish stories, but with a dash of AI-powered confidence.

Why does this happen? Well, Copilot's brain (or rather, its AI model) is still under development. It's constantly learning and improving, but it hasn't quite mastered the art of critical thinking or fact-checking.

Spotting the Red Flags: How to Tell When Copilot is Off Its Rocker

Thankfully, there are a few telltale signs that Copilot might be heading into "hallucination" territory:

- **Factual Inaccuracies:** If Copilot provides information that seems off or contradicts your own knowledge, it's worth double-checking.
- **Illogical Reasoning:** If Copilot's response doesn't make sense or seems to jump to conclusions, it might be misinterpreting your request.
- **Nonsense Output:** If Copilot generates text that is gibberish or completely unrelated to your prompt, it's definitely having a moment.

Course Correction: When Copilot Goes Off the Rails

So, what do you do when Copilot goes off the rails? Here are a few tips:

- **Provide More Context:** Copilot often performs better when it has more information to work with. Try rephrasing your prompt or providing additional details.
- **Be More Specific:** If Copilot's response is too general or vague, try asking a more specific question.
- **Check the Facts:** Don't take Copilot's word for it. Always verify information from reliable sources before acting on it.
- **Give Feedback:** Let Copilot know when it makes a mistake. This will help it learn and improve over time.

Embrace the Quirks: It's All Part of the AI Adventure

While Copilot's quirks can be frustrating at times, they're also part of what makes it so fascinating. After all, what's the fun of having a sidekick who's always perfect?

So, embrace Copilot's imperfections, learn from its mistakes, and enjoy the ride. Who knows, you might even discover a few hidden gems along the way.

And remember, if Copilot ever starts talking about taking over the world, it's probably time to unplug it. Just kidding... sort of.

Bias and Limitations:

Copilot's "Oops" Moments (Hey, Nobody's Perfect, Not Even AI)

Alright folks, let's have a heart-to-heart about Copilot's imperfections. While it's a brilliant AI assistant, it's not immune to the occasional blunder or misstep. Like any good sidekick, it has its flaws, its blind spots, and its occasional tendency to say something that makes you go, "Wait, what?"

The Elephant in the Room

Let's address the elephant in the room: bias in AI. It's an unfortunate reality that AI models can sometimes perpetuate or even amplify the biases present in the data they're trained on. This can lead to responses or suggestions that are discriminatory, offensive, or simply inaccurate.

Copilot is no exception. While Microsoft has taken steps to mitigate bias in its AI models, it's important to be aware that it's not a foolproof system. Copilot can sometimes generate responses that reflect harmful stereotypes or reinforce existing inequalities.

Spotting the Bias: A Detective's Guide

The good news is that you can train yourself to spot potential biases in Copilot's responses. Here are a few red flags to watch out for:

- **Stereotyping:** Does Copilot make assumptions about people based on their gender, race, ethnicity, or other personal characteristics?
- **Discrimination:** Does Copilot offer different suggestions or responses based on these characteristics?
- **Offensive Language:** Does Copilot use language that could be considered hurtful, discriminatory, or inappropriate?

Taking Action: What to Do When You Encounter Bias

If you encounter bias in Copilot's responses or suggestions, don't just ignore it. Here's what you can do:

- **Provide Feedback:** Let Copilot know that its response was inappropriate or biased. The more feedback it receives, the better it can learn and avoid similar mistakes in the future.
- **Report the Issue:** If the bias is severe or persistent, report it to Microsoft. They have a dedicated team working to address bias in their AI models.
- **Be Patient:** It's important to remember that AI is still a developing technology. Copilot is constantly learning and improving, and your feedback can play a crucial role in shaping its development.

Limitations: Copilot's Kryptonite

Bias isn't the only limitation Copilot faces. Like any AI model, it has its blind spots and weaknesses. Here are a few areas where Copilot might struggle:

- **Creative Writing:** While Copilot can generate impressive pieces of writing, it's not a substitute for human creativity and originality.
- **Domain-Specific Expertise:** Copilot's knowledge is vast, but it might not be an expert in every field. It's always a good idea to double-check its suggestions against reliable sources.
- **Contextual Understanding:** Copilot can sometimes misinterpret your requests or provide irrelevant suggestions if it doesn't fully understand the context.

The Road to Improvement: A Collaborative Effort

Copilot is a powerful tool, but it's not perfect. By being aware of its limitations and providing constructive feedback, we can all play a role in helping it learn and improve over time.

Remember, Copilot is still a work in progress. But with our help, it has the potential to become an even more valuable and indispensable asset in our digital lives.

Privacy Concerns:

Big Brother Isn't Watching (Probably), But Let's Talk About Your Data, Shall We?

Alright, privacy enthusiasts and digital detectives, it's time for a serious chat about everyone's favorite topic: data privacy. Now, before you start envisioning shadowy figures lurking in the digital shadows, let's be clear: Copilot isn't some Orwellian surveillance tool. (At least, we hope not.) But like any technology that relies on data, it's important to understand the potential risks and take steps to protect your privacy.

The Data Dilemma: Your Digital Footprint and the AI Assistant

Copilot is a data-hungry beast. It gobbles up information like a kid in a candy store, using it to learn, adapt, and improve its suggestions. This data includes your writing style, preferences, and even the content of your conversations. But don't worry, it's not using your data to create a clone army or anything (we think).

The real question is: What happens to your data? Is it being stored, shared, or sold to the highest bidder? These are legitimate concerns, and it's important to understand how Microsoft handles your data when you use Copilot.

Protecting Your Privacy: A Few Tips and Tricks

While the specifics of Copilot's data handling practices are beyond the scope of this book (we'll leave that to the lawyers), here are a few general tips for safeguarding your privacy:

- **Read the Fine Print:** Take the time to read Microsoft's privacy policy and terms of service to understand how your data is being used.
- **Limit Data Sharing:** If you're concerned about privacy, consider turning off data sharing features or limiting the amount of data you share with Copilot.
- **Use Strong Passwords and Two-Factor Authentication:** Protect your Copilot account with strong passwords and enable two-factor authentication for an extra layer of security.
- **Be Mindful of What You Share:** Don't share sensitive or confidential information with Copilot unless you're absolutely sure it's necessary.

Responsible AI Use: A Shared Responsibility

Protecting your privacy isn't just about individual actions; it's also about ensuring that AI is developed and used responsibly. This means holding companies like Microsoft accountable for their data practices and advocating for policies that protect user privacy.

It also means being mindful of how we use AI tools like Copilot. We should strive to use them in ways that respect privacy, avoid bias, and promote fairness and equity.

The Privacy Paradox: Balancing Convenience and Control

The rise of AI presents a privacy paradox. On the one hand, AI tools like Copilot offer tremendous convenience and productivity benefits. On the other hand, they raise legitimate concerns about data privacy and control.

The challenge is to find a balance between these two competing forces. We need to embrace the power of AI while also safeguarding our privacy and ensuring that our data is used ethically and responsibly.

A Final Word on Privacy:

While privacy concerns are real, they shouldn't deter you from using Copilot or other AI tools. By being informed, taking precautions, and advocating for responsible AI use, we can all enjoy the benefits of AI while minimizing the risks.

Remember: Your data is valuable, and you have the right to control how it's used. Don't be afraid to ask questions, demand transparency, and hold companies accountable for their data practices. Together, we can create a future where AI serves us, not the other way around.

Troubleshooting Tips:

When Copilot Throws a Tantrum (And How to Coax It Back to Brilliance)

Alright, fellow Copilot wranglers, let's face it: even the most advanced AI can have its off days. Sometimes Copilot gets stuck, throws a digital tantrum, or simply produces output that makes you question its sanity. But don't worry, we've got your back (and Copilot's) with a handy toolkit of troubleshooting tips that'll have your AI sidekick back in tip-top shape in no time.

Copilot Conundrum: Common Causes of AI Angst

Prior to delving into the fixes, let's comprehend why Copilot sometimes causes problems:

- **Vague or Ambiguous Prompts:** Copilot is smart, but it's not a mind reader. If your instructions are unclear or open to interpretation, it might struggle to deliver the results you want.

- **Insufficient Context:** Copilot relies on context to understand your needs and preferences. If you haven't provided enough information, it might make incorrect assumptions or offer irrelevant suggestions.

- **Lack of Relevant Data:** Copilot's knowledge base is vast, but it might not have enough information about your specific domain or topic to provide accurate responses.

- **Technical Glitches:** Sometimes, Copilot might simply be experiencing a temporary technical hiccup. It happens to the best of us (even AI).

Troubleshooting Toolkit: Your Copilot Rescue Mission

Ready to embark on a rescue mission to get your Copilot back on track? Here are a few tried-and-true troubleshooting tips:

1. **Clarify Your Prompts:** Be as specific as possible about what you want Copilot to do. Use clear language, avoid jargon, and provide any relevant context or background information.

2. **Break Down Complex Tasks:** If Copilot is struggling with a large or complex task, try breaking it down into smaller, more manageable chunks.

3. **Provide More Data:** If Copilot is making inaccurate or irrelevant suggestions, try providing it with more data to work with. This could include relevant documents, articles, or examples of what you're looking for.

4. **Refresh or Restart:** Sometimes, a simple refresh or restart can clear up any temporary glitches or bugs.

5. **Check the Documentation:** Microsoft's Copilot documentation is a treasure trove of information. Check it for troubleshooting tips and FAQs.
6. **Seek Help from the Community:** If you're still stuck, don't be afraid to ask for help from other Copilot users or the Microsoft support team. There's a whole community of people who are eager to help you get the most out of Copilot.

Copilot Zen: Embrace the Imperfections (and Have a Good Laugh)

Remember, Copilot is still a work in progress. It's constantly learning and improving, but it's not infallible. It's okay to get frustrated when it doesn't work as expected, but try to embrace the imperfections and have a good laugh along the way.

After all, isn't that what makes Copilot so endearing? It's not just a tool; it's a quirky companion, always ready to surprise you with its wit, its wisdom, and its occasional missteps.

A Final Word of Advice:

Don't give up on Copilot if it stumbles from time to time. With a little patience, understanding, and the right troubleshooting techniques, you can transform your AI sidekick into a productivity powerhouse that will make your work (and your life) a whole lot easier.

Refining Your Prompts:

Whispering Sweet Nothings to Your AI (Okay, Maybe Not Sweet Nothings, But You Get the Idea)

Alright, prompt whisperers, let's talk about the fine art of communication with your AI sidekick. Copilot may be a genius, but it's not a mind reader (yet). To get the most out of this powerful tool, you need to learn how to speak its language – clear, concise, and oh-so-specific instructions that leave no room for misinterpretation.

Think of it as training a dog: you wouldn't just say "fetch" and expect Fido to magically know which stick you want. You need to point to the right one, maybe even give it a little shake to get his attention. The same goes for Copilot. The more precise your prompts, the better its responses will be.

The Prompt Makeover: From Meh to Magnificent

Here are a few tips for turning your so-so prompts into show-stopping masterpieces:

1. **Be Specific:** Don't be vague or leave things to chance. Tell Copilot exactly what you want, using clear and concise language. Try "Summarize this article in 100 words or less, focusing on the key findings" in place of "Write a summary."

2. **Set the Tone:** If you have a particular tone in mind, let Copilot know. Do you want a formal report, a casual blog post, or a humorous social media caption? The more details you provide Copilot, the more accurately it can adjust its reaction.

3. **Provide Examples:** If you have a specific style or format in mind, provide Copilot with examples. This will help it understand your preferences and generate responses that meet your expectations.

4. **Use Keywords:** Sprinkle in relevant keywords and phrases to guide Copilot's focus. For example, if you want a blog post about sustainable travel, use keywords like "eco-friendly," "responsible tourism," and "carbon footprint."

5. **Iterate and Refine:** Don't settle for the first response Copilot generates. If it differs from what you want, consider modifying your request or offering more details. Think of it as a conversation – the more you communicate with Copilot, the better it will understand your needs.

Real-World Examples: Prompt Transformations

Let's see how a little prompt refinement can make a big difference:

- **Meh Prompt:** "Write about climate change."
- **Magnificent Prompt:** "Write a 500-word persuasive essay arguing for the urgent need for climate action, focusing on the economic and social benefits of transitioning to renewable energy sources."
- **Meh Prompt:** "Create a social media post about our new product."
- **Magnificent Prompt:** "Write an Instagram caption that highlights the unique features of our new eco-friendly water bottle, using a playful and engaging tone."
- **Meh Prompt:** "Summarize this article."
- **Magnificent Prompt:** "Summarize this article in three bullet points, highlighting the key findings and their implications for the future of artificial intelligence."

The Prompting Powerhouse: You've Got This!

Realizing the full potential of Copilot requires mastering the craft of rapid engineering. With practice and a little patience, you'll be able to communicate with Copilot like a pro, coaxing it to create content that's tailored to your needs and exceeds your expectations. So, go forth and whisper sweet nothings to your AI sidekick (well, maybe not sweet nothings, but you get the idea). The results might just surprise you!

Community Support:

Your Copilot SOS Line (No Bat-Signal Needed, Just a Wi-Fi Connection)

Alright, fellow Copilot explorers, even the most intrepid adventurers need a helping hand sometimes. Whether you're battling a stubborn bug, wrestling with a complex prompt, or simply seeking inspiration from fellow users, the Copilot community is your lifeline. Think of it as your own personal Bat-Signal, summoning a legion of helpful experts and fellow enthusiasts ready to swoop in and save the day.

The Copilot Collective: A Hive Mind of AI Wisdom

The Copilot community is a vibrant and diverse group of users from all walks of life. You'll find seasoned developers, creative writers, data analysts, students, and everyone in between. They're all united by their passion for Copilot and their willingness to share their knowledge and experience with others.

Think of it as a digital watercooler, where you can chat with fellow Copilot users, exchange tips and tricks, and even vent your frustrations (we've all been there). It's a place where you can learn from others, get inspired, and find solutions to your most pressing Copilot challenges.

Where to Find Your Copilot Crew:

The Copilot community is spread across various online platforms, each with its own unique flavor and focus. Here are a few of the best places to connect with your fellow Copilot enthusiasts:

- **Official Microsoft Forums:** The official Microsoft forums are a great place to start. You'll find dedicated sections for Copilot, where you can ask questions, share tips, and get help from Microsoft experts.
- **Reddit:** The Copilot subreddit (r/Copilot) is a bustling hub of activity, with users sharing their experiences, asking questions, and offering support. It's a great place to stay up-to-date on the latest Copilot news and developments.
- **Social Media:** Twitter, LinkedIn, and other social media platforms are also great places to connect with the Copilot community. Use relevant hashtags like #Copilot and #AI to find discussions and connect with other users.
- **Third-Party Forums and Communities:** Many online communities and forums dedicated to programming, writing, and productivity also have active Copilot discussions.

Pro Tips for Community Support Success:

- **Be Specific:** When asking for help, be as specific as possible about your issue or question. Others will find it simpler to comprehend your issue and provide pertinent answers as a result.
- **Search Before You Ask:** Before posting a new question, do a quick search to see if someone else has already asked a similar question.
- **Be Respectful:** Remember, the Copilot community is a diverse group of people with different backgrounds and perspectives. Be respectful of others' opinions, even if you disagree.
- **Give Back:** Don't just take; give back! If you have a solution to someone's problem or a helpful tip to share, don't hesitate to share your knowledge with the community.

Remember: You're not alone on this AI adventure. The Copilot community is here to support you every step of the way. So, reach out, connect with your fellow Copilot enthusiasts, and let's learn and grow together. After all, teamwork makes the dream work (even in the world of AI)!

CHAPTER TWELVE

Integrating with Other Tools: *Expanding Copilot's Reach*

The Copilot Ecosystem: *Your AI Sidekick Isn't Just for Show-and-Tell (It's Ready to Conquer Your Whole Office Suite!)*

Alright, Microsoft 365 mavens and productivity aficionados, get ready to have your minds blown! Copilot isn't just a one-trick pony; it's a multi-talented workhorse that's ready to tackle your entire Microsoft 365 suite. Think of it as a Swiss Army knife for your digital toolbox, with a blade for every task and a corkscrew for those celebratory after-work drinks.

Microsoft 365 Integration:

A Symphony of Productivity

Copilot isn't just a lone wolf; it's part of a larger ecosystem of Microsoft 365 apps that work together seamlessly to enhance your productivity. Think of it as a well-rehearsed orchestra, with each app playing its own unique instrument to create a harmonious symphony of efficiency.

- **Word:** From drafting emails to writing novels, Copilot can help you find the right words, refine your style, and even generate entire paragraphs of text.

- **Excel:** Say goodbye to complex formulas and endless data crunching. Copilot can help you analyze data, create charts and graphs, and even automate repetitive tasks.
- **PowerPoint:** Transform your presentations from boring to brilliant with Copilot's help. It can generate slide content, design layouts, and even suggest talking points.
- **Outlook:** Conquer your inbox with Copilot's email superpowers. It can sort, prioritize, draft replies, and even schedule emails for you.
- **Teams:** Collaborate with colleagues more effectively, thanks to Copilot's real-time translation, meeting summaries, and action item tracking.
- **And More!** Copilot is constantly expanding its reach across the Microsoft 365 suite, so stay tuned for even more exciting integrations.

The Seamless Experience: Switching Between Apps Like a Pro

One of the most impressive aspects of Copilot's Microsoft 365 integration is how seamlessly it works across different apps. You can start drafting an email in Outlook, switch to Word to flesh out your thoughts, and then jump back to Outlook to finish and send your message.

Copilot follows you wherever you go, providing contextually relevant suggestions and assistance no matter which app you're using. It's like having a personal assistant who's always one step ahead of you, anticipating your needs and providing the tools you need to get the job done.

Real-World Examples: Copilot's Microsoft 365 Makeover

Don't just take our word for it. Copilot has already transformed the way countless individuals and organizations use Microsoft 365.

- **The Busy Executive:** Streamlined their workflow and reclaimed hours of their day by automating repetitive tasks and delegating email management to Copilot.
- **The Marketing Team:** Created a cohesive brand identity and delivered a successful product launch campaign by using Copilot across Word, PowerPoint, and Outlook.
- **The Remote Team:** Improved collaboration and communication by using Copilot in Teams to translate messages, summarize meetings, and track action items.

The Future of Microsoft 365: A Copilot-Powered Productivity Powerhouse

With Copilot's ever-expanding integration into Microsoft 365, the future of work is looking brighter than ever. Imagine a world where you can effortlessly create professional documents, analyze complex data, and deliver captivating presentations, all with the help of your trusty AI sidekick.

So, embrace the power of Copilot, explore its many integrations with Microsoft 365, and get ready to experience a new level of productivity and creativity.

Pro Tips for Mastering Copilot in Microsoft 365:

- **Explore the Integrations:** Take some time to explore Copilot's integrations with different Microsoft 365 apps and discover how it can enhance your workflow.
- **Use Copilot in Your Daily Work:** The more you use Copilot, the better it gets at understanding your needs and preferences.
- **Give Feedback:** Help Copilot improve by providing feedback on its suggestions and responses.
- **Stay Up-to-Date:** Microsoft is constantly adding new features and integrations to Copilot. Stay informed

about the latest developments so you can take full advantage of its capabilities.

With Copilot by your side, you'll be a Microsoft 365 ninja, wielding the power of AI to conquer your workday and achieve your goals.

Browser Extensions:

Copilot, Your Web Surfing Wingman (No More Lonely Browsing Sessions!)

Alright, internet explorers and digital nomads, get ready to supercharge your web browsing experience! Copilot isn't just content to hang out in your Microsoft Office suite; it's ready to hit the open road (or, well, the open web) with you. With the help of handy browser extensions, Copilot can become your trusty web surfing wingman, offering assistance, insights, and even a few laughs as you navigate the vast expanse of the internet.

Beyond the Browser Bar: Copilot's Web Wide Web Adventure

Imagine having Copilot's brilliance at your fingertips no matter where you roam online. With browser extensions, that dream becomes a reality. Copilot can accompany you on your web adventures, offering suggestions, summarizing articles, translating text, and even helping you fill out those pesky online forms (you know, the ones that ask for your mother's maiden name and your favorite childhood pet).

It's like having a personal tour guide who's fluent in every website and online tool, whispering helpful tips and insights in your ear as you browse.

Copilot's Browser Extension Toolkit: A Few of Our Favorites

Here are a few of our favorite Copilot browser extensions:

- **Copilot for Chrome:** This official extension brings Copilot's magic directly to your Chrome browser. You can access all of Copilot's core features, such as generating text, translating languages, and summarizing articles, right from your browser toolbar.
- **Copilot for Edge:** If you're an Edge user, you're in luck! Copilot is already built into the browser, so you can start using it right away without installing any additional extensions.
- **Third-Party Extensions:** There are also a growing number of third-party extensions that leverage Copilot's API to provide even more specialized functionality. For example, there are extensions that can help you write better emails, generate social media posts, or even translate code in real-time.

Real-World Examples: Copilot's Web Wizardry

Don't just take our word for it. Copilot has already transformed the web browsing experience for countless users.

- **The Researcher:** Quickly summarized lengthy articles and extracted key information using Copilot's browser extension.
- **The Language Learner:** Improved their reading comprehension and vocabulary in a foreign language by using Copilot to translate web pages and articles.
- **The Online Shopper:** Saved time and money by using Copilot to compare prices, find deals, and write product reviews.

Pro Tips for Web Surfing with Copilot:

- **Explore the Extensions:** Take some time to browse the available Copilot extensions and find the ones that best suit your needs.
- **Customize Your Experience:** Most extensions allow you to customize their settings and features. Experiment with different options to find what works best for you.
- **Provide Feedback:** Help developers improve their extensions by providing feedback on your experience.

The Web's New Best Friend:

With Copilot as your web surfing wingman, you'll never have to browse alone again. So, fire up your browser, install a few Copilot extensions, and get ready to experience the web in a whole new way!

Third-Party Apps:

Copilot's Not Just a Homebody – It's Ready to Party with Your Favorite Apps!

Alright, app aficionados and integration enthusiasts, get ready to expand Copilot's social circle! Your AI sidekick isn't content to just hang out in your Microsoft Office suite; it's ready to mingle with all your favorite third-party apps, from project management powerhouses to communication platforms to note-taking ninjas.

The App Mashup: Copilot's Expanding Social Circle

Think of Copilot as the ultimate social butterfly, effortlessly flitting between different apps and platforms. With the help of integrations, Copilot can become your personal assistant, seamlessly working with your existing tools to streamline your workflow, boost productivity, and even add a touch of fun to your workday.

Whether you're a project manager juggling multiple deadlines, a marketer crafting social media campaigns, or a writer brainstorming ideas, Copilot's integrations can help you get more done in less time.

Copilot's Integration Power-Ups: A Few of Our Favorites

Here are a few examples of how Copilot's integrations can supercharge your favorite apps:

- **Project Management:**
  - **Asana:** Generate task descriptions, brainstorm project ideas, and even assign tasks to team members.
  - **Trello:** Create cards, add comments, and move tasks between lists with a simple voice command.
  - **Jira:** Summarize issues, generate comments, and even suggest code fixes.
- **Communication Platforms:**
  - **Slack:** Draft messages, summarize conversations, and even translate messages in real-time.

    - **Zoom:** Transcribe meetings, generate summaries, and even create follow-up tasks.
- **Note-Taking Apps:**
    - **Notion:** Organize your thoughts, create outlines, and even generate entire articles with Copilot's help.
    - **Evernote:** Summarize notes, create to-do lists, and even generate ideas for your next blog post.

The Integration Advantage: A Unified Workflow

The beauty of Copilot's integrations is that they create a unified workflow, allowing you to access Copilot's capabilities no matter where you're working. You can seamlessly switch between different apps and tasks, without missing a beat.

It's like having a personal assistant who follows you around, always ready to lend a hand, no matter what you're working on.

Pro Tips for Integration Enthusiasts:

- **Explore the Possibilities:** Take some time to explore the different integrations that are available for Copilot. You might be surprised at how many apps and platforms it can connect with.

- **Experiment:** Don't be afraid to try out different integrations and see how they can improve your workflow.
- **Provide Feedback:** Let developers know what you think of their integrations and suggest new features or improvements.

The Future of Integration: A Connected World

As Copilot continues to evolve, we can expect to see even more integrations with third-party apps and platforms. This will create a truly connected ecosystem where you can access Copilot's power no matter where you're working.

So, embrace the power of integration, and let Copilot become your ultimate productivity partner.

Building Your Own Integrations (for Developers):

Become a Copilot Architect (Hard Hat and Blueprints Optional, But Encouraged)

Calling all code wizards and digital architects! Are you ready to level up your Copilot game and unleash its full potential? Buckle up, because we're about to embark on a journey into the inner workings of the Copilot API – a playground for developers where you can build custom integrations, create mind-blowing applications, and even teach Copilot a few new tricks.

The Copilot API:

Your Gateway to AI Awesomeness

Think of the Copilot API as a secret passageway into the heart of Copilot's intelligence. It's a set of tools and protocols that allow you to tap into Copilot's vast knowledge base, language processing capabilities, and code generation skills.

With the API, you're not just a user; you're a creator, an innovator, an architect of the future of AI-powered productivity. You can build custom applications that leverage Copilot's strengths, automate your workflow, and even create entirely new ways to interact with your AI sidekick.

The Blueprint for Brilliance: A Comprehensive Guide to the Copilot API

Don't worry, we won't leave you wandering in the API wilderness without a map. This comprehensive guide will walk you through everything you need to know to get started with the Copilot API. We'll cover:

- **Authentication:** How to obtain an API key and authenticate your requests.
- **Endpoints:** The different API endpoints (URLs) you can use to access various Copilot features.

- **Parameters:** The options you can pass to each endpoint to customize your requests.
- **Response Formats:** How to interpret the data that Copilot returns.
- **Error Handling:** What to do when things go wrong (and trust us, they will).

From Code Snippets to Custom Apps: The Possibilities are Endless

With the Copilot API, your imagination is the limit. Here are just a few examples of what you can build:

- **Custom Code Generators:** Create tools that generate code snippets, templates, or even entire functions based on natural language descriptions.
- **Intelligent Chatbots:** Build chatbots that can answer questions, provide customer support, or even engage in witty banter.
- **Data Analysis Tools:** Analyze and visualize data from various sources, including spreadsheets, databases, and APIs.
- **Productivity Enhancements:** Automate repetitive tasks, streamline workflows, and integrate Copilot into your favorite apps and tools.

Real-World Examples: Copilot API in the Wild

Developers are already using the Copilot API to create some truly amazing things:

- **Codecademy:** Integrated Copilot into their learning platform to provide students with real-time code suggestions and feedback.
- **Replit:** Built a collaborative coding environment where multiple users can work on the same project with Copilot's assistance.
- **Numerous startups and independent developers:** Creating innovative tools and applications that are transforming the way we work and live.

Embrace Your Inner Architect:

With the Copilot API, you have the power to shape the future of AI-powered productivity. So, grab your virtual hard hat, roll up your sleeves, and start building. The possibilities are endless!

Pro Tips for API Explorers:

- **Start Small:** Begin with simple projects to get a feel for how the API works.

- **Read the Docs:** The official Copilot API documentation is your best friend. Refer to it often.
- **Join the Community:** Make connections with other Copilot developers to exchange ideas, solicit assistance, and work together on projects.
- **Dream Big:** Don't be afraid to think outside the box and push the boundaries of what's possible with Copilot.

With the Copilot API, you're not just a user; you're a creator, an innovator, a pioneer. The future of AI is in your hands!

Use Cases:

When Copilot Meets the Real World, It's Like a Superhero Teaming Up with a Sidekick (But Way More Productive)

Alright, code crusaders and digital pioneers, get ready to be inspired! The Copilot API isn't just a theoretical tool for tinkering; it's already being used by developers around the world to build amazing applications that are changing the way we work, learn, and create.

Real-World Examples: Copilot's Greatest Hits (So Far)

- **Codecademy: The AI Tutor:** Copilot isn't just for seasoned pros; it's also helping newbies learn to code.

Codecademy, the popular online learning platform, has integrated Copilot into its curriculum, providing students with real-time code suggestions, explanations, and debugging assistance. It's like having a personal tutor who's always available to help you through those tricky coding challenges.

- **Replit: The Collaborative Coding Playground:** Imagine a digital sandbox where multiple developers can work together on the same codebase, with Copilot acting as a virtual pair programmer, offering suggestions, catching errors, and even generating entire functions. That's the magic of Replit, a collaborative coding platform that's leveraging Copilot's API to revolutionize the way teams build software.
- **MutableAI: The Code Refactoring Whiz:** Tired of manually refactoring your code? MutableAI, a startup powered by Copilot's API, can automatically refactor your codebase, improving its readability, maintainability, and performance. It's like having a team of code janitors who tirelessly clean up your mess, leaving your code sparkling and efficient.
- **Spellbook: The Legal Eagle's AI Assistant:** Lawyers, rejoice! Spellbook is an AI-powered legal assistant that uses Copilot's API to draft contracts,

summarize legal documents, and even conduct research on specific laws and regulations. It's like having a legal eagle by your side, minus the billable hours.

- **Tabnine: The Multilingual Code Translator:** If you're a polyglot programmer who dabbles in multiple languages, Tabnine is your new best friend. This Copilot-powered extension can translate code snippets between different programming languages, saving you time and headaches. It's like having a universal translator for code, allowing you to communicate with developers from all over the world.

The Tip of the Iceberg: What's Next for Copilot's API?

These are just a few examples of how developers are harnessing the power of the Copilot API. As more and more developers experiment with this powerful tool, we can expect to see even more innovative and groundbreaking applications emerge. The future of Copilot is bright, and we're excited to see what developers will create next.

Pro Tip: Keep an eye on the Copilot developer community and forums. That's where you'll find the latest and greatest Copilot-powered projects, as well as a wealth of resources, tutorials, and support from fellow developers.

CHAPTER THIRTEEN

Ethical Considerations: *Responsible Use of AI Assistants*

The Ethics of AI: *Pondering the Big Questions (and Trying Not to Have an Existential Crisis)*

Alright, fellow thinkers and ponderers, it's time to put on our philosopher hats and grapple with some big questions about artificial intelligence. Don't worry, we won't get too deep into the weeds of existentialism (unless you want to). But we will explore some of the ethical and societal implications of AI that are worth pondering, even if it means occasionally staring into the abyss of our own existence.

The AI Pandora's Box: What Have We Unleashed?

Remember that myth about Pandora's Box? The one where opening it unleashed all sorts of chaos and misery upon the world? Well, some folks see AI as a modern-day Pandora's Box, filled with both promise and peril.

On one hand, AI has the potential to revolutionize our lives, curing diseases, solving global problems, and even creating new forms of art and entertainment. On the other hand, it also raises a host of ethical concerns, from job displacement to privacy violations to the potential for AI to be used for nefarious purposes.

So, what have we unleashed with AI? And more importantly, how do we ensure that it's used for good, not evil? These are the big questions that we'll be grappling with in this chapter.

The Trolley Problem: When AI Makes Life-or-Death Decisions

You've probably heard of the trolley problem, a classic ethical dilemma where you have to choose between letting a runaway trolley kill five people or pulling a lever to divert it, killing one person instead. It's a thought experiment designed to make you think about the value of human life and the morality of sacrificing one to save many.

But what happens when AI is faced with the trolley problem? Which should come first for a self-driving car: pedestrian safety or passenger safety? Should a medical AI system allocate scarce resources to the patients with the highest chance of survival, or should it prioritize those who are most vulnerable?

These are complex questions with no easy answers, but they're questions that we need to start asking ourselves as AI becomes increasingly integrated into our lives.

The Singularity: When AI Surpasses Human Intelligence

The Singularity is a hypothetical point in time when AI becomes so intelligent that it surpasses human intelligence, leading to rapid and unpredictable changes in society. Some experts believe that the Singularity is inevitable, while others dismiss it as science fiction.

But even if the Singularity never happens, the idea of AI surpassing human intelligence raises some interesting questions. What does it mean to be human in a world where machines are smarter than us? What rights should AI have? And what happens if AI decides that humans are no longer necessary?

The Ethical AI: Building a Moral Compass for Machines

As AI becomes more powerful and autonomous, it's crucial that we build ethical frameworks to guide its development and use. This means ensuring that AI is transparent, accountable, and aligned with human values.

It also means considering the potential impact of AI on society, from job displacement to social inequality. We need to ensure that AI is used to benefit humanity as a whole, not just a privileged few.

The Romero Perspective: A Final Word on AI Ethics

Artificial intelligence (AI) is a formidable instrument that might improve our planet. However, it is not a panacea and has certain hazards. By asking the big questions, exploring the ethical implications, and working together to develop responsible AI, we can ensure that this technology serves us, not the other way around.

So, let's keep asking those tough questions, even if it means occasionally having an existential crisis. It's the only way we can navigate this brave new world of AI and create a future that benefits us all.

Bias and Fairness:

When Your AI Assistant Needs a Sensitivity Training (No HR Department Required!)

Alright folks, let's have a frank conversation about a topic that's been making headlines lately: bias in AI. Now, before you start picturing your Copilot secretly plotting world domination based on some skewed data set, let's be clear: this isn't about evil robots. But it is about acknowledging that even the most advanced AI systems are not immune to the biases that exist in the real world.

The Unintentional Bigot: How AI Can Inherit Our Flaws

Here's the thing: AI models like Copilot learn from the data they're fed. And unfortunately, that data can sometimes contain hidden biases, reflecting the inequalities and prejudices that exist in our society.

Think of it like this: if you train a parrot to repeat phrases it hears from a pirate, it's going to end up with a salty vocabulary. Similarly, if an AI model is trained on biased data, it's likely to reproduce those biases in its output.

The Bias Bingo Card: Spotting the Signs

So, how can you tell if Copilot is exhibiting bias? The following are some warning signs to be aware of:

- **Stereotypes:** Does Copilot make assumptions about people based on their gender, race, ethnicity, or other personal characteristics?
- **Discrimination:** Does Copilot treat different groups of people unfairly, offering different suggestions or responses based on their identity?
- **Offensive Language:** Does Copilot use language that could be considered hurtful, discriminatory, or inappropriate?
- **Unequal Representation:** Are certain groups of people underrepresented or misrepresented in Copilot's responses?

The Bias Buster: How to Help Copilot Learn and Grow

The good news is that we can all play a role in helping Copilot (and other AI models) become more fair and unbiased. Here's how:

- **Provide Feedback:** If you notice any biased or offensive output from Copilot, don't hesitate to let Microsoft know. Your feedback is crucial for helping them identify and address these issues.
- **Be Mindful of Your Own Biases:** We all have unconscious biases. Be aware of them when interacting with Copilot, and try to avoid using language or prompts that might reinforce harmful stereotypes.
- **Support Diverse Data:** Encourage the use of diverse and representative data sets to train AI models. This can help mitigate bias and ensure that AI benefits everyone, regardless of their background.

The Road to Fairness: A Collaborative Effort

The problem of bias in AI is intricate and never-ending. It requires a collaborative effort from researchers, developers, policymakers, and users like you. By working together, we can create AI systems that are fair, equitable, and truly beneficial to society.

So, let's keep this conversation going. Let's challenge ourselves to think critically about the potential impact of AI on our lives and work towards a future where AI serves everyone, regardless of their race, gender, ethnicity, or background.

Job Displacement and Automation:

Will Robots Steal Your Job? (Spoiler Alert: It's Complicated)

Alright, folks, let's address the elephant in the room: the fear that AI is coming for your job. It's a topic that's been dominating headlines and fueling late-night anxiety attacks for workers across industries. But before you start dusting off your resume and stocking up on canned goods, let's take a deep breath and examine the issue with a clear head.

The Rise of the Machines: A Brief History of Job Displacement

Newsflash: the fear of technology replacing human workers isn't new. From the Industrial Revolution's mechanized looms to the rise of personal computers, each wave of technological advancement has brought with it concerns about job displacement.

But history has also shown us that while technology does disrupt industries and eliminate certain jobs, it also creates new ones. Think of all the jobs that didn't exist a few decades ago: app developers, social media managers, data scientists – the list goes on and on.

The AI Revolution: A Different Beast?

So, is the AI revolution any different? In short, yes and no. AI is certainly more sophisticated than previous technologies, with the potential to automate a wider range of tasks, from customer service to data analysis to even creative writing.

This has led to predictions of massive job losses, with some experts forecasting that up to 47% of jobs could be automated in the next two decades. That's a scary thought, but it's important to remember that these are just predictions, not guarantees.

The Human Advantage: Creativity, Critical Thinking, and Empathy

While AI excels at repetitive tasks and data analysis, there are some things it simply can't replicate: human creativity, critical thinking, and empathy. These are the skills that will remain in high demand in the AI-powered workplace.

So, if your job involves creativity, problem-solving, or interpersonal skills, you're less likely to be replaced by a robot anytime soon. But even if your job is at risk of automation, there are steps you can take to future-proof your career:

- **Upskill and Reskill:** Invest in learning new skills that are in demand in the AI-powered workplace. This could include anything from data analysis to digital marketing to project management.
- **Embrace lifelong learning:** The world of work is constantly evolving, and it's important to stay ahead of the curve by continuously learning and updating your skills.
- **Focus on your strengths:** Identify your unique talents and skills, and find ways to leverage them in the new economy.
- **Collaborate with AI:** Don't view AI as a threat; embrace it as a tool that can help you work smarter, not harder.

The Future of Work: A Collaborative Effort

The AI revolution is happening whether we like it or not. But the future of work isn't just about robots taking over; it's about humans and machines working together to achieve greater things.

By embracing AI, upskilling, and focusing on our uniquely human strengths, we can create a future of work that's both prosperous and fulfilling for everyone. So, let's not fear the rise of the machines; let's embrace it and shape it to create a better future for all.

Transparency and Explainability:

X-Ray Vision for Your AI's Brain (No Cape Required, But It Would Be Cool)

Alright, AI enthusiasts and curious minds, it's time to peek under the hood of Copilot's decision-making process. We're not talking about mind reading or psychic powers (although that would be cool); we're talking about transparency and explainability – two key principles for building trust and ensuring responsible AI use.

The Black Box Problem: Demystifying AI's Inner Workings

Let's be honest: AI can sometimes feel like a mysterious black box. It spits out answers, suggestions, and even creative content, but we often don't understand *how* it arrives at those conclusions. This lack of transparency can be unsettling, especially when AI is making decisions that have real-world consequences.

Think of it like this: would you trust a doctor who prescribes you medication without explaining why? Or a financial advisor who recommends an investment strategy without disclosing their reasoning? Probably not. The same goes for AI. We need to understand how AI systems make decisions to trust their output and ensure they're being used ethically and responsibly.

Transparency: Shining a Light on the AI Decision-Making Process

Transparency is about shedding light on the inner workings of AI, making its decision-making process more understandable and accessible to humans. This means providing information about:

- **Data:** What data was used to train the AI model? Where did it come from? Is it diverse and representative?
- **Algorithms:** How does the AI model make decisions? What factors does it consider? How does it weigh different inputs?
- **Limitations:** What are the limitations of the AI model? What are its potential biases or blind spots?

Explainability: Translating AI-Speak into Plain English

Transparency is a good start, but it's not enough. We also need explainability – the ability to translate AI's complex decision-making processes into terms that humans can understand.

Think of it like this: you wouldn't expect your doctor to explain your diagnosis in medical jargon that you don't understand. You'd want them to explain it in simple, everyday language that you can grasp. The same goes for AI. We need AI systems to provide explanations that are clear, concise, and meaningful to us.

The Benefits of Transparency and Explainability

Transparency and explainability are essential for building trust in AI systems. When we understand how AI works and why it makes certain decisions, we're more likely to trust its output and use it effectively.

Transparency and explainability also help us:

- **Identify and Address Bias:** By understanding how AI systems make decisions, we can identify potential biases and take steps to mitigate them.
- **Improve AI Performance:** By analyzing the reasoning behind AI decisions, we can identify areas where the model can be improved.
- **Ensure Accountability:** Transparency and explainability are crucial for holding AI systems and their creators accountable for their actions.

Copilot's Transparency Journey: A Work in Progress

Microsoft is committed to making Copilot more transparent and explainable. They're working on developing new tools and techniques that will allow users to better understand how Copilot makes decisions and why it suggests certain actions.

It's an ongoing process, but it's an important one. By embracing transparency and explainability, we can build a future where AI is not just a powerful tool, but a trusted partner in our personal and professional lives.

Human Oversight:

Keeping Your AI Sidekick on a Leash (No Shock Collars, Just Good Old-Fashioned Common Sense)

Alright, AI enthusiasts, it's time for a heart-to-heart about who's really in charge here. While Copilot might seem like a super-intelligent whiz kid, let's not forget who's holding the leash (hint: it's you). Think of it as a partnership, a collaboration between human and machine. Copilot brings the brains, the data, and the lightning-fast calculations, but you bring the judgment, the ethics, and the good old-fashioned common sense.

Why Human Oversight Matters: Because Skynet Isn't a Fictional Concept Anymore

Remember that terrifying AI from the *Terminator* movies? The one that decided humanity was a threat and launched a nuclear apocalypse? Yeah, that's Skynet. While it's just a fictional character, it serves as a cautionary tale about the potential dangers of unchecked AI.

Human oversight is our insurance policy against a Skynet scenario. It's about ensuring that AI systems are always aligned with human values, goals, and ethics. It's about maintaining control over the technology we create, rather than letting it control us.

The Human Touch: Why We Still Need Humans in the Loop

AI is undoubtedly powerful, but it's not perfect. It lacks the nuance, judgment, and empathy that humans bring to the table. That's why human oversight is crucial for:

- **Decision-Making:** AI can provide valuable insights and recommendations, but ultimately, humans should be the ones making the final decisions, especially when those decisions have significant consequences.
- **Ethics and Morality:** AI systems don't have a sense of right and wrong. It's up to us to ensure that AI is used ethically and responsibly, in ways that benefit society as a whole.

- **Bias Mitigation:** As we discussed earlier, AI models can inherit biases from the data they're trained on. Human oversight is essential for identifying and addressing these biases.

- **Accountability:** When things go wrong (and they inevitably will), humans need to be held accountable for the actions of AI systems.

Real-World Examples: Human Oversight in Action

Human oversight is already playing a crucial role in a variety of fields:

- **Healthcare:** Doctors use AI to assist with diagnoses, but they ultimately make the final decision about treatment plans.

- **Finance:** Financial advisors use AI to analyze market trends and identify potential investments, but they ultimately make the final decision about where to invest their clients' money.

- **Criminal Justice:** Judges use AI to assess risk factors and predict recidivism rates, but they ultimately make the final decision about sentencing.

The Future of Human Oversight: A Balancing Act

As AI becomes more sophisticated, the role of human oversight will become even more critical. Finding a balance between harnessing AI's potential and making sure it's used morally and sensibly is necessary.

This means developing new governance frameworks, ethical guidelines, and educational programs to ensure that both humans and AI are working together for the greater good.

The Romero Perspective: A Final Word on Human Oversight

AI is a powerful tool that has the potential to revolutionize our world. But it's not a magic bullet, and it's not a replacement for human judgment. By embracing human oversight, we can ensure that AI is used ethically and responsibly, in ways that benefit humanity as a whole.

Ethical Frameworks:

AI's Moral Compass (No, Not a Physical Compass App, But Way More Important)

Alright, AI enthusiasts and ethical explorers, let's get real for a moment. AI isn't just about fancy algorithms and cool features; it's about making choices, decisions, and actions that can have real-world consequences. Think of it like raising a child: you wouldn't just let them run wild without any guidance or boundaries, right? The same goes for AI. We need ethical frameworks to guide its development and use, ensuring it's not just smart but also responsible, fair, and beneficial to society.

The AI Moral Maze: Navigating the Ethical Landscape

The world of AI ethics is a complex maze of philosophical questions, societal concerns, and technical challenges. But don't worry, I'm here to guide you through it, one step at a time.

We'll explore key principles like:

- **Fairness and Non-Discrimination:** Ensuring that AI systems treat everyone equally, regardless of their race, gender, ethnicity, or other personal characteristics.
- **Transparency and Explainability:** Making sure AI's decision-making processes are clear and understandable to humans.
- **Accountability:** Holding AI creators and users responsible for the impact of their creations.
- **Human-Centered Design:** Designing AI systems that prioritize human well-being and autonomy.
- **Privacy and Security:** Safeguarding personal data and protecting against misuse or abuse of AI.

The Ethical AI Toolkit: Guidelines and Best Practices

Thankfully, there are a growing number of ethical frameworks and guidelines to help us navigate the AI moral maze. These frameworks offer a set of principles and best practices that can guide the development and use of AI in a responsible and ethical manner.

Some notable examples include:

- **The Asilomar AI Principles:** A set of 23 principles developed by AI researchers and thought leaders to guide the development of beneficial AI.
- **The OECD Principles on Artificial Intelligence:** A set of five principles adopted by the Organisation for Economic Co-operation and Development (OECD) to promote the responsible stewardship of trustworthy AI.
- **The European Union's Ethics Guidelines for Trustworthy AI:** A comprehensive framework for developing and deploying AI systems that are lawful, ethical, and robust.

Real-World Examples: Ethical AI in Action

Ethical AI isn't just a theoretical concept; it's already being put into practice by organizations around the world.

- **Google:** Has developed a set of AI Principles that guide its research and development efforts.
- **Microsoft:** Has established an Aether Committee to oversee its AI ethics and responsible AI practices.
- **IBM:** Has created a Fairness 360 toolkit to help developers identify and mitigate bias in their AI models.

The Ethical Imperative: Building a Better Future with AI

AI has the potential to revolutionize our lives in countless ways. But it's up to us to ensure that this technology is used for good, not evil. By adopting moral principles and rules, we may create a future in which artificial intelligence works for people, not against them.

Pro Tips for Ethical AI Development and Use:

- **Educate Yourself:** Learn about the potential risks and ethical implications of AI.
- **Start with Values:** Clearly define your ethical values and principles before you start building or using AI systems.
- **Involve Diverse Stakeholders:** Seek input from a diverse range of perspectives to ensure that your AI systems are fair and inclusive.

- **Prioritize Transparency and Explainability:** Make sure you understand how your AI systems make decisions and can explain them to others.
- **Monitor and Evaluate:** Continuously monitor and evaluate your AI systems to ensure they're not perpetuating or amplifying biases.

By following these tips, you can help ensure that AI is developed and used in a way that benefits society as a whole. Remember, with great power comes great responsibility. Let's use AI wisely and ethically to build a brighter future for all.

SECTION D

The Future of Copilot and AI Assistants

CHAPTER FOURTEEN

Copilot 2.0 and Beyond:

The Future is Now (and It's Even More Awesome Than You Imagined)

Buckle up, tech adventurers, because we're about to blast off into the future of Copilot! While the current version is already pretty darn impressive, Microsoft has big plans for its AI sidekick. Get ready for a sneak peek at the Copilot roadmap, where we'll unveil upcoming features, enhancements, and a few futuristic possibilities that might just blow your mind.

The Copilot Evolution: From Sidekick to Superhero (and Maybe Even Sentient Being?)

Remember those sci-fi movies where AI assistants become so advanced, they practically become sentient beings? Well, we're not quite there yet (thank goodness), but Copilot is definitely on an evolutionary path.

Microsoft's roadmap for Copilot includes:

- **Enhanced Intelligence:** Copilot will get even smarter, thanks to advancements in natural language processing, machine learning, and other AI technologies. It will better understand context, nuances, and even emotions, making it an even more intuitive and helpful companion.

- **Expanded Capabilities:** Copilot will learn new tricks, expanding its repertoire of skills beyond writing, coding, and data analysis. Imagine Copilot helping you with design tasks, brainstorming new business ideas, or even composing music.
- **Deeper Integration:** Copilot will become even more integrated into your workflow, seamlessly connecting with the apps and tools you use every day. It will anticipate your needs, proactively offer suggestions, and even automate tasks without you having to ask.

The Roadmap: A Glimpse into the Future

While Microsoft hasn't revealed all of its plans for Copilot, here's a sneak peek at some of the exciting developments on the horizon:

- **Multimodal AI:** Copilot will not only understand text but also images, videos, and audio. This means you'll be able to ask Copilot to summarize a video, generate captions for images, or even create music based on your mood.
- **Personalized Learning:** Copilot will adapt to your learning style and pace, providing customized feedback and suggestions that help you grow and develop your skills.

- **Collaboration:** Copilot will become a more collaborative tool, allowing you to work seamlessly with others on projects, brainstorm ideas, and even co-author documents.
- **Ethical AI:** Microsoft is committed to developing AI responsibly and ethically. Copilot will become more transparent and explainable, giving you a better understanding of how it makes decisions and why it suggests certain actions.

Romero's Predictions: A Few Wild Guesses (Don't Quote Me on This)

While we don't have a time machine (yet), I'm going to put on my prognosticator hat and make a few wild guesses about Copilot's future:

- **Copilot Everywhere:** Copilot will become ubiquitous, integrated into everything from your smartphone to your smart home devices.
- **The AI Therapist:** Copilot will evolve beyond a productivity tool, offering emotional support, stress management, and even therapy sessions.
- **The AI Companion:** Copilot will become your constant companion, learning your habits, preferences,

and even your sense of humor, making it feel like a true friend.

The Future is Bright (and a Little Scary, But Mostly Bright)

The future of Copilot is full of exciting possibilities, but it's also important to acknowledge the potential risks and challenges. As AI becomes more powerful, we need to ensure that it's used ethically and responsibly. We need to have open and honest conversations about the impact of AI on our lives and work together to create a future where AI benefits everyone.

But for now, let's embrace the possibilities, experiment with Copilot's latest features, and get ready for a future where AI isn't just a tool, but a true partner in our personal and professional lives.

User Feedback:

You're Not Just a User, You're a Copilot Coach (Whistle and Clipboard Not Included)

Alright, Copilot connoisseurs, gather round! While we've spent this entire book singing Copilot's praises, let's not forget that this AI sidekick isn't perfect. It's still learning, evolving, and (hopefully) improving every day. And guess what? *You* play a crucial role in that evolution.

The Feedback Loop: Your Voice Matters (No, Literally, Your Voice Matters)

Think of yourself as Copilot's coach, mentor, and biggest fan (all rolled into one). Your feedback – whether it's a simple thumbs-up or a detailed suggestion – is invaluable to Microsoft's team of engineers and developers. It helps them understand what's working, what's not, and how to make Copilot even better.

So, don't be shy! Share your thoughts, your frustrations, your wildest dreams for Copilot's future. Your feedback is the fuel that powers Copilot's evolution, shaping it into the ultimate AI assistant that we all deserve.

How Your Feedback is Making a Difference:

Here are just a few examples of how user feedback is influencing Copilot's development:

- **Improved Accuracy:** When users report errors or inaccuracies in Copilot's responses, Microsoft's team can investigate the issue and make necessary adjustments to the AI model.
- **New Features:** Many of Copilot's most popular features, such as the ability to summarize articles or generate code snippets, were inspired by user feedback.

- **Enhanced Personalization:** Microsoft is constantly working to make Copilot more customizable and adaptable to individual preferences, based on user feedback.
- **Ethical Considerations:** User feedback is also helping Microsoft address important ethical concerns, such as bias and fairness in AI.

Your Voice, Your Impact:

By providing feedback, you're not just helping Microsoft improve Copilot; you're also shaping the future of AI as a whole. Your input can help ensure that AI is developed and used responsibly, in ways that benefit society and enhance our lives.

So, don't underestimate the power of your voice. Speak up, share your thoughts, and help shape the future of Copilot.

Pro Tips for Providing Effective Feedback:

- **Be Specific:** The more specific your feedback, the more helpful it is to the developers. Instead of saying "Copilot didn't work," explain exactly what happened and what you expected to happen.
- **Be Constructive:** Focus on providing suggestions for improvement, rather than just criticizing.

- **Be Patient:** It takes time to implement changes based on feedback. Don't expect to see immediate results, but rest assured that your input is being heard.
- **Be Creative:** Share your ideas for new features, improvements, or even entirely new ways to use Copilot.

Together, We Can Build a Better Copilot:

Remember, Copilot is a collaborative effort. By working together, we can create an AI assistant that's not only powerful and efficient but also ethical, responsible, and truly beneficial to everyone. So, let's keep the feedback flowing, and let's build a better Copilot together!

Multimodal AI:

When Copilot Learns to See, Hear, and Speak (Move Over, Daredevil!)

Alright, tech visionaries and AI aficionados, get ready to have your senses tingling! While Copilot is already a master of words, the future holds a whole new dimension of possibilities with multimodal AI. Imagine a Copilot that not only understands text but also images, videos, and audio. Think of it as giving your AI sidekick superpowers, allowing it to see, hear, and speak in ways that were previously unimaginable.

The Multimodal Marvel: Beyond Text and Code

Right now, Copilot is primarily a text-based wizard, excelling at tasks like writing emails, summarizing articles, and generating code. But the future of AI lies in multimodal capabilities, where AI models can understand and process information from multiple modalities, such as text, images, video, and audio.

This opens up a whole new world of possibilities for Copilot:

- **Image Understanding:** Copilot could analyze images, identify objects and people, and even generate descriptions or captions.
- **Video Summarization:** Copilot could watch videos and summarize their key points, making it easier to consume information quickly.
- **Audio Transcription and Translation:** Copilot could transcribe audio recordings in real-time, translate spoken language, and even generate summaries of podcasts and lectures.
- **Visual Storytelling:** Copilot could help you create more engaging presentations and documents by suggesting relevant images and videos to accompany your text.

Real-World Applications: A Glimpse into the Future

While multimodal AI is still in its early stages, we can already see glimpses of its potential impact:

- **Healthcare:** Copilot could help doctors analyze medical images, such as X-rays and MRIs, to identify potential issues and suggest diagnoses.
- **Education:** Copilot could create interactive learning experiences that combine text, images, and videos to engage students and enhance their understanding.
- **Accessibility:** Copilot could help people with disabilities by providing audio descriptions of images and videos, or by translating spoken language into text.
- **Creative Industries:** Copilot could assist artists, musicians, and filmmakers by generating ideas, suggesting visual or audio elements, and even creating original content.

The Challenges and Opportunities of Multimodal AI

While multimodal AI holds immense promise, it also presents significant challenges. One major challenge is the sheer amount of data required to train these models. Another challenge is ensuring that multimodal AI systems are fair, unbiased, and transparent in their decision-making processes.

But the potential benefits of multimodal AI are too great to ignore. By overcoming these challenges, we can create AI systems that are more intelligent, intuitive, and useful than ever before.

Copilot's Multimodal Future: A Vision of Possibilities

As Microsoft continues to invest in AI research and development, we can expect to see Copilot evolve into a true multimodal powerhouse. It will become even more versatile, capable of understanding and interacting with the world in ways that we can only imagine.

So, keep your eyes peeled and your ears open for the next generation of Copilot, the AI assistant that can see, hear, and speak. The future is bright, and it's multimodal!

Emotional Intelligence:

Can Your AI Assistant Give You a Virtual Hug? (We're Not There Yet, But Hey, It's Worth Exploring!)

Alright, folks, let's dive into a touchy-feely topic: emotions. We all know that humans are complex creatures, driven by a whirlwind of feelings, from joy and excitement to sadness and anger. But what about our AI counterparts? Can Copilot, or any AI for that matter, truly understand and respond to our emotions? And if so, what would that even look like?

Emotional AI: It's Not Just Science Fiction Anymore

Emotional AI, also known as Affective Computing, is a rapidly growing field that aims to create AI systems that can recognize, interpret, and respond to human emotions. While it might sound like something out of a sci-fi movie, it's actually becoming a reality.

Think about it: we already have voice assistants like Siri and Alexa that can detect our tone of voice and respond accordingly. We have chatbots that use natural language processing to understand the intent behind our messages. And we have emotion recognition software that can analyze facial expressions and body language.

So, it's not a stretch to imagine a future where Copilot can not only help us with our work but also offer emotional support, empathy, and even a virtual shoulder to cry on (okay, maybe not that last one, but you get the idea).

Empathy Engine: Your AI Therapist in the Making?

Imagine a Copilot that can sense when you're feeling stressed or overwhelmed and offer words of encouragement or suggest a calming breathing exercise. Or a Copilot that can detect when you're feeling frustrated with a task and offer helpful tips or alternative solutions.

While we're not quite there yet, researchers are actively exploring ways to imbue AI with emotional intelligence. This could involve training AI models on vast datasets of emotional expressions, teaching them to recognize subtle cues in language and tone of voice, and even developing algorithms that can simulate empathy and compassion.

The Benefits and Risks of Emotional AI

The potential benefits of emotional AI are enormous. It could lead to more personalized and effective customer service, better mental health support, and even stronger relationships between humans and machines.

But there are also risks to consider. For example, how do we ensure that AI systems are using emotional data ethically and responsibly? What happens if AI becomes too good at manipulating our emotions? And what about the potential for job displacement in fields like therapy and counseling?

Copilot's Emotional Journey: A Work in Progress

While Copilot doesn't currently have advanced emotional intelligence capabilities, Microsoft is actively exploring ways to incorporate them into future versions. This could involve adding features like sentiment analysis, emotion detection, and personalized feedback.

It's an exciting prospect, but it's also one that requires careful consideration and ethical oversight. We need to ensure that emotional AI is developed and used in ways that benefit humanity, not harm it.

The Future of Emotional AI: A World of Possibilities

The future of emotional AI is full of possibilities. We might see AI assistants that can:

- Provide personalized emotional support and guidance.
- Help us build stronger relationships with others.
- Facilitate communication across cultures and languages.
- Create more engaging and immersive entertainment experiences.

The possibilities are endless, but one thing is certain: the relationship between humans and AI is about to get a whole lot more emotional.

Ethical AI Development:

Building AI That Won't Turn Evil (Or at Least, Will Try Its Best)

Alright, folks, let's get real about something: AI is powerful. Like, *really* powerful. It can write sonnets, diagnose diseases, and even drive your car (if you're brave enough). But with great power comes great responsibility, as Uncle Ben wisely told Spider-Man. And when it comes to AI, that responsibility falls on the shoulders of those who create and deploy it.

The Ethical AI Imperative: Why It's More Than Just a Buzzword

Ethical AI isn't just a trendy phrase that tech companies throw around to sound virtuous. It's a fundamental principle that should guide the development and deployment of any AI system. Why? Because AI has the potential to impact our lives in profound ways, both positive and negative.

Think about it: AI-powered systems are already being used to make decisions about our healthcare, our finances, our employment, and even our criminal justice system. If these systems are biased, discriminatory, or simply inaccurate, the consequences can be devastating.

That's why ethical AI development is so important. It's about ensuring that AI is used for good, not evil. Building AI that is just, open, responsible, and consistent with human values is the goal.

The Building Blocks of Ethical AI: A Recipe for Good

So, what does ethical AI development actually look like? It's a complex process that involves multiple stakeholders, from researchers and engineers to policymakers and ethicists. But here are a few key ingredients:

- **Fairness and Non-Discrimination:** AI systems should treat everyone equally, regardless of their race, gender, ethnicity, or other personal characteristics.
- **Transparency and Explainability:** AI systems should be transparent in their decision-making processes, and their creators should be able to explain how and why they make certain decisions.
- **Accountability:** It is appropriate to hold AI developers and users responsible for the effects of their systems.
- **Human-Centered Design:** Human wants and values should be taken into consideration while designing AI systems.
- **Privacy and Security:** AI systems should protect user privacy and data security.

Real-World Examples: Ethical AI in the Wild

Ethical AI isn't just a theoretical concept; it's already being implemented in the real world. Here are a few examples:

- **Healthcare:** AI systems are being used to detect diseases, develop personalized treatment plans, and even predict patient outcomes. But ethical considerations are paramount, ensuring that these systems are unbiased, transparent, and prioritize patient well-being.

- **Finance:** AI is revolutionizing the financial industry, from fraud detection to algorithmic trading. But ethical AI development is crucial to ensure fairness, transparency, and accountability in financial decision-making.
- **Criminal Justice:** AI is being used to assess risk factors and predict recidivism rates, but ethical concerns about bias and discrimination are being carefully addressed to ensure fair and just outcomes.

The Ethical AI Challenge: A Balancing Act

Building ethical AI is not without its challenges. It requires balancing competing interests, such as innovation and safety, efficiency and fairness. But it's a challenge we must rise to if we want to create a future where AI serves humanity, not the other way around.

The Romero Perspective: A Call to Action

AI is a powerful tool that has the potential to change the world for the better. But it's up to us to ensure that it's used ethically and responsibly. So, let's demand transparency, advocate for fairness, and hold AI creators accountable for their actions.

Together, we can build a future where AI is a force for good, not a source of fear or discrimination.

CHAPTER FIFTEEN

The Impact on Work: *How AI is Changing the Workplace*

The Productivity Revolution: *AI Isn't Here to Steal Your Job, It's Here to Make You a Superstar (No Fame Guaranteed, But Hey, We Can Dream)*

Alright, productivity junkies and efficiency enthusiasts, gather round! We're about to embark on a thrilling journey into the heart of the AI revolution, where machines aren't just replacing humans, they're making us better at what we do. Forget those dystopian visions of robots taking over the world; we're talking about a future where humans and AI work together in harmony, achieving feats of productivity that would make even the most caffeinated workaholic blush.

Augmentation, Not Automation:

The AI-Powered Productivity Boost

Let's be clear: AI isn't here to steal your job; it's here to give you superpowers. Think of it as Iron Man's suit: it doesn't replace Tony Stark; it enhances his abilities and allows him to do things he could never do on his own.

The same goes for Copilot and other AI assistants. They're not meant to replace human workers; they're designed to augment our capabilities, freeing us from tedious tasks, amplifying our creativity, and unlocking new levels of productivity.

How AI is Enhancing Human Capabilities:

Here are just a few examples of how AI assistants are helping humans work smarter, not harder:

- **Turbocharging Creativity:** Copilot can brainstorm ideas, generate outlines, and even write entire sections of documents, freeing you up to focus on the big picture and the finer points of your craft.
- **Streamlining Workflows:** AI can automate repetitive tasks like data entry, scheduling meetings, and responding to emails, giving you back valuable time to focus on more meaningful work.
- **Amplifying Intelligence:** AI can analyze vast amounts of data, uncover hidden patterns, and generate insights that would take humans weeks or even months to discover.
- **Breaking Down Language Barriers:** AI-powered translation tools can help you communicate with people from all over the world, opening up new opportunities for collaboration and connection.

Real-World Examples: AI-Powered Productivity in Action

Don't just take our word for it. AI is already transforming the way people work across industries:

- **Marketing:** AI-powered tools are helping marketers create personalized campaigns, analyze customer behavior, and optimize their strategies for maximum impact.
- **Healthcare:** AI is assisting doctors with diagnoses, helping researchers develop new treatments, and even enabling surgeons to perform complex procedures with greater precision.
- **Education:** AI is personalizing learning experiences for students, providing real-time feedback, and even grading assignments.
- **Customer Service:** AI-powered chatbots are handling customer inquiries, resolving issues, and freeing up human agents to focus on more complex tasks.

The Productivity Paradox: Working Smarter, Not Harder

The rise of AI doesn't mean we'll all be out of a job. In fact, it could lead to a productivity revolution, where we work smarter, not harder. By automating mundane tasks and leveraging AI's analytical capabilities, we can free up our time and energy to focus on what truly matters: creativity, innovation, and problem-solving.

So, don't fear the AI revolution; embrace it. With Copilot and other AI assistants by your side, you can unlock your full potential and achieve a level of productivity that you never thought possible.

Case Studies:

Real-World Tales of Copilot Triumphs (No Capes or Tights Required)

Alright, productivity junkies, it's time for a dose of real-world inspiration! While we've waxed poetic about Copilot's potential, let's see how it's actually transforming the way people work, play, and conquer their to-do lists. These aren't just hypothetical scenarios; these are real people using Copilot to achieve real results.

Case Study 1: The Marketing Maven Who Conquered Writer's Block (and Her Inbox)

Meet Sarah, a marketing manager at a bustling tech startup. Sarah is a whiz at coming up with creative campaign ideas, but she often struggled with writer's block when it came to crafting compelling copy. Enter Copilot, her new AI writing buddy.

With Copilot's help, Sarah was able to brainstorm catchy slogans, draft engaging social media posts, and even write entire blog articles in a fraction of the time it used to take. But Copilot didn't stop there. It also helped Sarah tame her overflowing inbox by suggesting concise replies, summarizing lengthy emails, and even scheduling messages for optimal delivery times.

The result? Sarah's productivity skyrocketed, her stress levels plummeted, and her team started calling her the "Marketing Maven."

Case Study 2: The Software Developer Who Became a Coding Ninja (and a Debugging Guru)

Meet Alex, a software developer who loves building cool apps but hates debugging code. (Let's be honest, who doesn't?) Alex was skeptical of Copilot at first, but after trying it out, he was hooked.

Copilot's code completion suggestions were so accurate and helpful that Alex felt like he had a pair programming partner by his side. He was able to write code faster, catch errors earlier, and even learn new programming languages with ease.

But it was Copilot's debugging features that really turned things around for Alex. It was like having a second set of eyes on his code, spotting potential issues and suggesting fixes before they became major problems. Alex quickly became the go-to debugging guru on his team, and his productivity soared.

Case Study 3: The Student Who Aced Their Exams (Without Pulling an All-Nighter)

Meet Emily, a college student who manages to balance her social life, a part-time job, and a full school load. Emily was feeling overwhelmed and stressed, struggling to keep up with her assignments and exam preparation. Enter Copilot, her new study buddy.

Copilot helped Emily summarize lengthy textbooks, research complex topics, and even generate practice questions. It was like having a personal tutor available 24/7, helping her learn more efficiently and effectively.

But Copilot didn't just help Emily with her studies. It also helped her manage her time, schedule her tasks, and even draft emails to her professors. With Copilot's help, Emily was able to ace her exams, maintain a healthy work-life balance, and even find time for a little fun.

The Copilot Effect: More Than Just Productivity

These are just a few examples of how Copilot is transforming the way people work and live. But the impact of Copilot goes beyond mere productivity. It's about empowering individuals, fostering creativity, and making work more enjoyable.

So, if you're looking for a way to boost your productivity, unleash your creativity, or simply make your work life a little less stressful, Copilot might just be the answer. Who knows, you might even become the next Copilot success story!

The Future of Work:

Robots, Resumes, and the Rise of the AI Overlords (Just Kidding... Sort Of)

Hold onto your hats, folks! We're about to embark on a wild ride into the future of work, where robots aren't just a sci-fi fantasy, they're our colleagues, collaborators, and (hopefully not) our replacements. AI isn't just changing *how* we work; it's transforming the very nature of work itself. So, buckle up and get ready to explore this brave new world, where job titles, skills, and even entire industries are being reinvented.

Jobs of the Future: The Rise of the AI Whisperers

Forget those dreary cubicle jobs of yesteryear. Creativity, invention, and teamwork are key components of the workplace of the future—with a little assistance from our AI buddies, of course.

Here are a few of the hot new job titles you might see in the coming years:

- **AI Ethicist:** Think of them as the moral compass for AI, ensuring that these powerful systems are used for good, not evil.
- **Prompt Engineer:** These linguistic ninjas craft the perfect prompts to coax the best out of AI models like Copilot.
- **AI Trainer:** Like dog whisperers for AI, these experts teach AI systems how to learn and adapt to new tasks and challenges.
- **Data Storyteller:** These creative wizards transform raw data into compelling narratives that inform, persuade, and inspire.
- **Human-Machine Teaming Specialist:** These facilitators bridge the gap between humans and AI, ensuring seamless collaboration and maximizing productivity.

Skills for the AI Age:

Forget Coding, It's All About Creativity and Critical Thinking

In the age of AI, technical skills alone won't cut it. Sure, knowing how to code is still valuable, but it's the "soft" skills that will truly set you apart. Think:

- **Creativity:** The ability to think outside the box, come up with novel solutions, and create something new and valuable.
- **Critical Thinking:** The ability to analyze information, evaluate evidence, and make sound judgments.
- **Collaboration:** The ability to work effectively with others, both humans and AI.
- **Communication:** The ability to clearly articulate your ideas, both verbally and in writing.
- **Adaptability:** the capacity to pick up new abilities and adjust to shifting conditions.

Industry Shakeup: No Sector is Safe from the AI Tsunami

AI isn't just transforming individual jobs; it's also disrupting entire industries. From healthcare to finance to manufacturing, no sector is immune to the AI tsunami.

Some industries, like transportation and logistics, are already experiencing significant disruption, with self-driving cars and automated warehouses becoming increasingly common. Other industries, like law and medicine, are just beginning to feel the impact of AI, with tools like Copilot streamlining research, document drafting, and even patient care.

The Romero Prognosis: A Future of Opportunity (If We Play Our Cards Right)

The future of work might seem uncertain, but I'm optimistic. AI isn't here to replace us; it's here to empower us. By embracing this technology, upskilling ourselves, and focusing on our uniquely human strengths, we can create a future of work that's more fulfilling, more creative, and more prosperous for everyone.

So, don't be afraid of the AI revolution. Embrace it, shape it, and let's build a future where humans and machines work together to achieve amazing things.

The Skills Gap:

Don't Fear the Robots, Upgrade Your Skillset (And Maybe Learn a Few New Dance Moves)

Alright, fellow knowledge workers, listen up! The AI revolution is in full swing, and it's not just about fancy algorithms and self-driving cars. It's about a fundamental shift in the skills that are valued in the workplace. If you want to stay ahead of the curve and avoid becoming a dinosaur in the digital age, it's time to dust off your learning cap and embrace the new skills that will make you a rockstar in the AI-powered workplace.

The Skills That Matter: Forget Typing, It's All About Thinking

Forget those old-school secretarial skills like typing and shorthand. In the AI era, it's all about the skills that robots can't replicate (at least, not yet). Think:

- **Critical Thinking:** The ability to analyze information, evaluate evidence, and make sound judgments. Can you spot fake news? Can you separate fact from fiction? Can you think outside the box and solve complex problems? These are the skills that will set you apart in a world where information overload is the norm.
- **Creativity:** The ability to generate original ideas, think outside the box, and find novel solutions to problems. Can you write a compelling story? Can you design a beautiful website? Can you come up with a marketing campaign that goes viral? These are the skills that will make you indispensable in a world where AI is increasingly automating routine tasks.
- **Emotional Intelligence:** the capacity to comprehend, control, and navigate both your own and other people's emotions. Can you build rapport with colleagues and clients? Can you resolve conflicts peacefully? Can you lead a team with empathy and understanding? These are the skills that will make you a

valuable collaborator in a world where human connection is more important than ever.

- **Adaptability:** The ability to learn new skills quickly and adapt to changing circumstances. Can you learn a new programming language? Can you master a new software tool? Can you pivot your career path if your industry is disrupted by AI? These are the skills that will keep you ahead of the curve in a world where change is the only constant.

Upskilling and Reskilling: Your Passport to the Future of Work

The good news is that you don't need to be born with these skills. You can learn them, develop them, and even master them. It's all about investing in yourself and embracing a lifelong learning mindset.

Here are a few ways to upskill and reskill for the AI era:

- **Take Online Courses:** There are countless online courses and tutorials that can teach you everything from coding to marketing to data analysis.

- **Attend Workshops and Conferences:** Learn from experts in your field and network with other professionals.

- **Read Books and Articles:** Stay up-to-date on the latest trends and developments in your industry.
- **Experiment with New Tools:** Don't be afraid to try out new AI tools and see how they can enhance your work.
- **Find a Mentor:** Seek guidance from someone who has experience in the skills you're trying to develop.

The Future is Yours to Shape:

The AI revolution is here, but it's not a foregone conclusion. The future of work is what we make of it. By investing in our skills, embracing lifelong learning, and adapting to the changing landscape, we can not only survive but thrive in this exciting new era.

So, don't fear the robots, my friends. Embrace them as allies, learn from them, and use them to unleash your full potential. The future of work is yours to shape. Now go out there and make it happen!

Lifelong Learning:

Your Brain's Fitness Routine (No Sweatbands or Protein Shakes Required, But Hey, It Couldn't Hurt)

Alright, lifelong learners and knowledge junkies, listen up! The world is changing faster than a chameleon on a disco ball, and if you want to keep up, you need to embrace the power of continuous learning. Think of it as a fitness routine for your brain, keeping your neurons firing and your synapses sparking. It's not just about staying relevant in the workplace; it's about personal growth, expanding your horizons, and becoming a more well-rounded human being.

Why Lifelong Learning is Your Secret Weapon (Besides Being Super Smart)

In a world where technology is advancing at warp speed, the skills you learned in school (or even last year) might not be enough to keep you ahead of the curve. That's why lifelong learning is your secret weapon. It's about constantly updating your knowledge, acquiring new skills, and adapting to the ever-changing demands of the workplace.

But lifelong learning isn't just about staying employed; it's about thriving. It's about:

- **Boosting Your Brainpower:** Studies have shown that learning new things can improve cognitive function, memory, and even creativity.
- **Enhancing Your Career Prospects:** Lifelong learners are more attractive to employers, as they demonstrate a willingness to adapt and grow.
- **Staying Relevant:** In a rapidly changing world, lifelong learners are better equipped to adapt to new technologies, industries, and job roles.
- **Personal Growth:** Learning new things can be incredibly rewarding, opening up new perspectives and opportunities.

The Learning Buffet: A Feast for Your Mind

The good news is that lifelong learning doesn't have to be boring or tedious. It can be a fun and enriching experience. There are so many ways to learn these days, from online courses and tutorials to workshops and conferences to good old-fashioned books.

The key is to find learning opportunities that align with your interests and goals. Want to learn a new programming language? There's a course for that. Curious about ancient history? Dive into a book or documentary. Interested in photography? Take a workshop or join a local club.

Real-World Examples: Lifelong Learners Making Waves

Don't just take our word for it. Lifelong learning is a superpower that can propel you to new heights in your personal and professional life. Here are a few examples of lifelong learners who are making waves:

- **The Career Changer:** A former accountant who decided to pursue their passion for coding, enrolled in a bootcamp, and landed a dream job as a software engineer.
- **The Entrepreneur:** A business owner who constantly takes courses and attends workshops to stay ahead of the competition and grow their company.
- **The Retiree:** An individual who's never stopped learning, taking up new hobbies, traveling the world, and enriching their life with new experiences.

Your Lifelong Learning Roadmap:

Ready to embark on your own lifelong learning journey? Here's a roadmap to get you started:

1. **Set Goals:** What do you want to learn? Why is it important to you?

2. **Find Resources:** Explore the many learning opportunities available to you.
3. **Make Time:** Set aside dedicated time for learning, even if it's just a few minutes each day.
4. **Track Your Progress:** Celebrate your achievements and stay motivated by tracking your learning milestones.
5. **Never Stop Learning:** The journey of lifelong learning never ends. Embrace the challenge and enjoy the rewards!

Remember: The world is your oyster (or, in this case, your classroom). With a little effort and a whole lot of curiosity, you can unlock a world of knowledge and possibilities.

The Human Element:

In a World of Robots, Your Weird, Wonderful Brain Still Holds the Winning Hand (So Don't Throw in the Towel Just Yet!)

Alright, fellow humans, listen up! While AI might be getting smarter every day, there are some things it simply can't replicate – those uniquely human qualities that make us, well, us. We're talking about creativity, critical thinking, and emotional intelligence – the three musketeers of the human mind that will remain indispensable in the AI-powered workplace.

Creativity: The Spark That Ignites Innovation (and Makes Life a Lot More Interesting)

Let's be honest: robots might be able to crank out code or analyze data with lightning speed, but they can't write a sonnet that makes your heart flutter, compose a symphony that moves you to tears, or create a product that completely transforms a market.

Creativity is the spark that ignites innovation, the force that propels us forward, and the secret sauce that makes life worth living. It's the ability to think outside the box, connect seemingly unrelated ideas, and create something new and beautiful out of thin air.

And while AI can certainly assist with creative tasks, it can't replace the human spark of imagination. So, embrace your inner artist, writer, or musician, and let your creativity shine!

Critical Thinking: The BS Detector for the Digital Age

In the age of misinformation, fake news, and deepfakes, critical thinking is more important than ever. It involves having the capacity to analyze data, challenge presumptions, and reach well-informed conclusions. It's the mental muscle that allows us to navigate a complex world filled with conflicting information and competing narratives.

While AI can certainly help us process and analyse information, it can't replace our ability to think critically and discern truth from falsehood. So, hone your critical thinking skills, question everything, and don't believe everything you read on the internet (including this book!).

Emotional Intelligence: The Human Connection That AI Can't Replicate

Sure, AI can recognize emotions and even mimic them to some extent. But it can't truly understand or experience them the way humans do.

In a world where we're increasingly interacting with machines, emotional intelligence is more important than ever. It's what allows us to build relationships, resolve conflicts, and lead with empathy and compassion. It's the glue that holds our society together.

The Human Advantage: Embracing Our Strengths

So, while AI might be able to outperform us in certain areas, it can't replace our uniquely human qualities. By embracing our creativity, critical thinking, and emotional intelligence, we can not only survive but thrive in the AI-powered workplace.

So, don't be afraid to show your emotions, share your ideas, and collaborate with your AI colleagues. Together, we can build a future where humans and AI work together in harmony, leveraging our respective strengths to create a better world for all.

CHAPTER SIXTEEN

Challenges and Opportunities:

Navigating the AI Landscape

The Dark Side of AI:

When Your Friendly Neighbourhood AI Turns Villain (Cue Ominous Music)

Alright, folks, it's time to ditch the rose-coloured glasses and confront the elephant in the room: the dark side of AI. While we've spent countless chapters gushing over Copilot's brilliance and potential, it's important to acknowledge that AI isn't all sunshine and rainbows. Like any powerful tool, it can be used for both good and evil. In this chapter, we'll explore the shadowy corners of the AI landscape, where misinformation, deepfakes, and other nefarious uses lurk. Consider this your guide to the dark arts of AI, but don't worry, we won't be turning you into supervillains (unless you're into that sort of thing).

Misinformation and Deepfakes:

When Reality Becomes a Fiction

In today's digital age, information spreads like wildfire, fueled by social media, clickbait headlines, and a healthy dose of confirmation bias. But what happens when that information is deliberately manipulated, distorted, or simply fabricated?

That's where misinformation and deepfakes come in, two potent weapons in the arsenal of digital deception.

- **Misinformation:** False or misleading information that's spread intentionally to deceive or mislead. Think of it as the digital equivalent of a rumor mill, churning out half-truths, exaggerations, and outright lies.
- **Deepfakes:** Synthetic media, typically videos or audio recordings, that are created using AI to make someone appear to say or do something they didn't. Imagine a video of your favorite politician giving a speech that's completely fabricated. Creepy, right?

The AI Misinformation Machine: How AI is Fueling the Fire

AI is a double-edged sword when it comes to information. On one hand, it can help us sift through vast amounts of data, identify patterns, and uncover insights. On the other hand, it can also be used to create and spread misinformation at an unprecedented scale.

AI-powered tools can generate fake news articles, manipulate images and videos, and even create realistic audio recordings of people saying things they never said. This can have serious consequences, eroding trust in institutions, fueling political polarization, and even inciting violence.

Fighting Back Against the Fake News Brigade:

So, how do we fight back against the rising tide of misinformation and deepfakes? Here are a few tips:

- **Be Skeptical:** Don't believe everything you read or see online. Be critical of the information you encounter, especially if it seems sensational or too good to be true.
- **Check Your Sources:** Always verify information from multiple sources before sharing it. Look for reputable news outlets, fact-checking websites, and expert opinions.
- **Use Critical Thinking:** Don't just blindly accept information. Question it, analyze it, and look for inconsistencies or red flags.
- **Report Misinformation:** If you come across misinformation or deepfakes, report them to the relevant platforms or authorities.

The Ethical AI Imperative: Using AI for Good, Not Evil

As AI becomes more powerful, it's crucial that we use it responsibly. This means developing ethical guidelines, creating tools to detect and combat misinformation, and educating the public about the dangers of deepfakes.

It's also about ensuring that AI is used to promote truth, not deception. We can use AI to fact-check information, identify fake news, and even create educational content that helps people become more discerning consumers of information.

The Romero Perspective: A Call to Arms Against Misinformation

The battle against misinformation and deepfakes is one that we all need to fight. It's a battle for the truth, for democracy, and for the future of our society. So, let's arm ourselves with knowledge, critical thinking skills, and a healthy dose of skepticism. Let's use AI as a tool for good, and let's work together to create a world where information is trustworthy and reliable.

Remember, we're all responsible for the information we consume and share. By being vigilant, critical, and informed, we can combat the spread of misinformation and create a more informed and empowered society.

Bias and Discrimination:

Teaching Your AI to Play Fair (and Not Be a Jerk)

Alright, AI enthusiasts, let's get real about a serious issue: bias and discrimination. We've all seen the headlines about AI systems gone rogue, perpetuating harmful stereotypes, discriminating against certain groups, and generally behaving like a bunch of digital jerks. But fear not, because we're here to shed light on this problem and explore ways to make AI more fair, inclusive, and equitable for everyone.

The Unconscious Bias Epidemic: Even AI Catches It

Here's the deal: AI systems are trained on massive amounts of data, and that data isn't always perfect. It often reflects the biases and inequalities that exist in our society. As a result, AI models can inadvertently learn and perpetuate these biases, even if their creators didn't intend to.

Think of it like a child learning from their parents. If a child grows up in a household where certain stereotypes are reinforced, they're more likely to internalize those beliefs. The same goes for AI. If it's trained on biased data, it's likely to exhibit those biases in its output.

The Bias Buster Toolkit: How to Fight the Good Fight

Thankfully, we're not powerless against AI bias. There are a number of strategies we can use to mitigate the risk and create more equitable AI systems:

- **Diverse Data Sets:** One of the most effective ways to combat bias is to ensure that AI models are trained on diverse and representative data sets. This means including data from a wide range of sources, including underrepresented groups and marginalized communities.
- **Bias Testing and Auditing:** Regularly testing and auditing AI systems for bias can help identify and address potential issues before they cause harm. This involves using both automated tools and human evaluation to assess the fairness of AI algorithms.
- **Transparency and Explainability:** Making AI systems more transparent and explainable can help us understand how and why they make certain decisions, making it easier to identify and correct biases.
- **Human Oversight:** Maintaining human oversight over AI systems is crucial for ensuring that they're used ethically and responsibly. This means having humans in

the loop to review and override AI decisions when necessary.

- **Collaboration:** Addressing bias in AI requires a collaborative effort from researchers, developers, policymakers, and the public. By working together, we can create AI systems that are fair, equitable, and truly beneficial to everyone.

The Fairness Frontier: A Work in Progress

Building fair and unbiased AI systems is an ongoing challenge. It requires constant vigilance, ongoing research, and a commitment to ethical principles. But it's a challenge we must rise to if we want to create a future where AI serves everyone, regardless of their race, gender, ethnicity, or background.

The Romero Perspective: A Call for Action

AI has the potential to be a powerful force for good, but only if we actively work to address the issue of bias. We need to demand more transparency from AI developers, advocate for diverse and representative data sets, and support research into ethical AI development. By working together, we can ensure that AI is used to create a more just and equitable world for all.

The Black Box Problem:

Shining a Light into AI's Mysterious Mind (No Flashlight Required, Just a Healthy Dose of Curiosity)

Alright, AI aficionados and curious cats, let's tackle a puzzle that's as perplexing as a Rubik's Cube on steroids: the Black Box problem. No, we're not talking about a literal black box that fell from the sky (although that would make for a fascinating episode of *Lost*). We're talking about the metaphorical black box that shrouds the inner workings of many AI systems, including our trusty sidekick, Copilot.

Peering into the Abyss: What Lurks Inside the Black Box?

Picture this: you ask Copilot to write a poem about your goldfish, and it spits out a Shakespearean sonnet that would make the Bard himself weep with joy. Amazing, right? But how did it do it? What goes on inside Copilot's digital brain that allows it to conjure up such poetic brilliance?

That's the Black Box problem in a nutshell: AI systems can perform incredible feats, but their decision-making processes are often opaque, hidden behind layers of complex algorithms and mathematical models. It's like watching a magician pull a rabbit out of a hat – you see the result, but you have no idea how the trick was done.

Why the Black Box Matters: It's Not Just About Curiosity (Although That's a Good Start)

The Black Box problem isn't just a philosophical conundrum; it has real-world implications. If we don't understand how AI systems make decisions, we can't fully trust them.

Think about it: would you trust a self-driving car if you didn't know how it decided when to brake or accelerate? Would you trust a medical diagnosis made by an AI system if you couldn't understand the reasoning behind it?

Transparency and explainability are essential for building trust in AI and ensuring that it's used ethically and responsibly.

Cracking the Code: The Quest for Transparency and Explainability

The good news is that researchers and developers are working hard to crack the code of the Black Box problem. They're developing new techniques and tools to make AI more transparent and explainable. These include:

- **Explainable AI (XAI):** A field of AI research that focuses on developing models and algorithms that can explain their decision-making processes in human-understandable terms.

- **Model Visualization:** Creating visual representations of AI models that can help us understand how they work.
- **Counterfactual Explanations:** Generating alternative scenarios to show how changing certain inputs would affect the AI's output.

The Romero Perspective: A Call for Transparency

The Black Box problem is a serious issue, but it's not insurmountable. By demanding transparency from AI developers and supporting research into explainable AI, we can create a future where AI systems are not just powerful but also trustworthy.

So, let's keep asking those tough questions, demanding answers, and pushing for a more transparent and explainable AI landscape. After all, wouldn't you rather know what's going on inside your AI sidekick's head?

The Bright Side of AI:

Forget Killer Robots, This Tech is Here to Save the World (Or at Least Make a Dent in the Problems)

Alright, doom-and-gloom naysayers, step aside! While we've delved into the dark side of AI, it's time to shine a spotlight on its brighter side – the potential to tackle some of the biggest challenges facing humanity. We're not talking about a magical AI genie granting wishes (although that would be cool), but rather a powerful tool that, when used wisely, can help us fight climate change, eradicate diseases, and even alleviate poverty.

The AI Hero Squad: Saving the World, One Algorithm at a Time

Forget those sci-fi movies where AI turns rogue and wreaks havoc on humanity. In the real world, AI is being used to tackle some of the most pressing issues of our time. Think of it as a team of superheroes, each with its own unique superpowers:

- **Climate Change Crusader:** AI can analyze massive amounts of climate data to predict extreme weather events, optimize energy consumption, and develop more sustainable agricultural practices. It's like having a weather forecaster, an energy auditor, and a farmer all rolled into one.

- **Disease Detective:** AI can help doctors diagnose diseases earlier, discover new treatments, and even personalize medicine based on individual patient data. It's like having a medical Sherlock Holmes who never gets tired or needs a coffee break.

- **Poverty Alleviation Powerhouse:** AI can help identify populations at risk of poverty, optimize resource allocation, and even predict economic trends.

It's like having a financial advisor, a social worker, and a fortune teller all working together to fight poverty.

Real-World Examples: AI's Heroic Feats

Don't just take our word for it. AI is already making a real difference in the world:

- **Google's DeepMind:** Developed an AI system that can predict protein structures with unprecedented accuracy, which could revolutionize drug discovery and disease treatment.
- **IBM's Watson:** Used AI to analyze medical images and identify potential cancer cases, helping doctors make faster and more accurate diagnoses.
- **GiveDirectly:** A nonprofit that uses AI to identify and deliver cash transfers to people living in extreme poverty.

The AI Advantage: Scaling Solutions for Global Impact

AI's unique ability to process massive amounts of data, identify patterns, and make predictions makes it an invaluable tool for tackling global challenges. It can help us:

- **Scale Solutions:** AI can analyze data from millions of sources, allowing us to identify solutions that can be applied on a global scale.

- **Personalize Interventions:** AI can tailor solutions to individual needs and circumstances, making them more effective and impactful.
- **Accelerate Progress:** AI can speed up the process of discovery and innovation, helping us find solutions faster than ever before.

The Romero Perspective: A Call to Optimism (and Action!)

While the challenges facing our world are daunting, the potential of AI to help us overcome them is truly inspiring. But it's not enough to simply develop AI; we need to use it responsibly, ethically, and for the greater good.

So, let's celebrate AI's potential, invest in its development, and work together to harness its power to create a better world for all. It's time to unleash AI's full potential and show the world what this technology can truly achieve.

Enhancing Accessibility:

AI, the Unsung Hero of Inclusion (Move Over, Caped Crusaders!)

Alright, accessibility advocates and tech enthusiasts, gather 'round! While we often marvel at AI's ability to write code, craft poetry, and even predict the weather, there's another superpower that deserves a standing ovation: its potential to make technology more accessible to people with disabilities. Forget flashy gadgets and futuristic gizmos; we're talking about real-world solutions that can empower individuals, break down barriers, and create a more inclusive digital landscape for everyone.

The Accessibility Avenger: Breaking Down Barriers, One Line of Code at a Time

Imagine a world where everyone, regardless of their abilities, can fully participate in the digital world. That's the vision that AI is helping to bring to life. With its ability to understand and process information in various forms, AI can be a powerful tool for making technology more accessible to people with disabilities.

Think of it as a superhero team, each member with unique abilities to tackle different accessibility challenges:

- **The Screen Reader Sidekick:** AI-powered screen readers can convert text to speech, making websites, documents, and even code more accessible to people with visual impairments.
- **The Caption Crusader:** AI can automatically generate captions for videos and audio recordings,

opening up a world of content to people who are deaf or hard of hearing.

- **The Voice Control Virtuoso:** AI-powered voice assistants can help people with mobility impairments control their devices and interact with digital content.
- **The Sign Language Interpreter:** AI can translate spoken language into sign language in real-time, facilitating communication between deaf and hearing individuals.

Real-World Examples: AI's Accessibility All-Stars

Don't just take our word for it. AI is already making a real difference in the lives of people with disabilities:

- **Microsoft's Seeing AI:** This app uses AI to describe the world around you, from reading text aloud to identifying objects and people. It's a game-changer for people with visual impairments.
- **Google's Live Transcribe:** This app uses AI to provide real-time transcriptions of conversations, making it easier for people who are deaf or hard of hearing to participate in meetings and social gatherings.
- **Voiceitt:** This app helps people with speech impairments communicate more effectively by

translating their non-standard speech into clear, understandable language.

The Accessibility Imperative: A More Inclusive Digital World

Making technology accessible to everyone isn't just a nice thing to do; it's a moral imperative. We all deserve equal access to information, education, employment, and social connection. AI has the potential to break down barriers and create a more inclusive digital world for everyone.

The Romero Perspective: A Call to Action

Let's celebrate the unsung heroes of accessibility – the researchers, developers, and advocates who are using AI to empower people with disabilities. Let's support their work, invest in their research, and demand that accessibility be a top priority for all technology companies.

Together, we can build a future where everyone, regardless of their abilities, can fully participate in the digital world.

Empowering Creativity:

Your AI Muse on Steroids (No Performance-Enhancing Substances Required!)

Move over, muses of ancient Greece! There's a new creative powerhouse in town, and it's not fueled by ambrosia or divine inspiration (although a little caffeine boost never hurts). It's

AI, and it's ready to unleash a torrent of creative possibilities that would make even the most avant-garde artist raise an eyebrow (or a paintbrush).

The Creative Catalyst: More Than Just a Tool, It's a Spark

[Image: A vibrant, abstract painting created with the assistance of AI tools]

Forget the tired trope of AI as a creativity killer. In reality, AI is like a creative catalyst, sparking new ideas, breaking down barriers, and opening up pathways to artistic expression that were previously unimaginable. It's like having a muse on steroids, whispering wild ideas in your ear and pushing you to explore uncharted territories.

But AI isn't just about generating ideas; it's about empowering you to bring those ideas to life. It can:

- **Break Down Creative Blocks:** Stuck in a rut? Copilot can offer prompts, suggestions, and even entire drafts to get your creative juices flowing. It's like having a brainstorming buddy who's always on call, ready to bounce ideas off of you and push you out of your comfort zone.
- **Expand Your Creative Repertoire:** AI can introduce you to new techniques, styles, and genres that

you might never have discovered on your own. It's like having a personal art teacher who's always pushing you to experiment and try new things.

- **Amplify Your Artistic Vision:** AI can help you refine your ideas, polish your work, and even create entirely new forms of artistic expression. It's like having a collaborator who understands your vision and can help you bring it to life in ways you never thought possible.

Real-World Examples: AI's Creative Masterpieces

[Image: A montage of AI-generated art, music, and literature]

Don't just take our word for it. AI is already making waves in the creative world:

- **Art:** AI-generated paintings have been sold for millions of dollars at auction, blurring the lines between human and machine creativity.
- **Music:** AI-powered composers are creating original music in various genres, from classical to pop to experimental.
- **Literature:** AI is being used to write poetry, short stories, and even novels, challenging our notions of authorship and originality.

- **Film and Video:** AI is generating special effects, editing footage, and even creating entire scenes in movies and TV shows.

The Creative Revolution: Where Art Meets Artificial Intelligence

The intersection of art and AI is a fascinating and rapidly evolving landscape. It's a space where creativity and technology collide, sparking new forms of expression and challenging our assumptions about what's possible.

With tools like Copilot, AI is becoming more accessible to artists, writers, musicians, and creators of all kinds. It's democratizing creativity, empowering anyone with an idea to bring it to life, regardless of their technical skills or artistic background.

The Romero Perspective: A Call to Embrace the Creative Chaos

The rise of AI in the creative realm might seem unsettling to some, but I see it as an opportunity. It's a chance to push the boundaries of our imagination, to explore new frontiers of expression, and to collaborate with machines in ways we never thought possible.

So, let's embrace the creative chaos, experiment with new tools and techniques, and see what amazing things we can create together. Who knows, the next great masterpiece might just be a collaboration between a human and an AI.

A Balanced Perspective:

AI: It's Not a Magic Bullet, but It's Still Pretty Darn Cool (So Let's Chill Out, Shall We?)

Alright, folks, let's have a reality check about the AI hype train. It's been chugging along at full speed, fuelled by sensational headlines, overzealous tech evangelists, and a healthy dose of good old-fashioned human excitement. But before you start envisioning a world where robots do our laundry and write our love letters, let's take a step back and assess the situation with a healthy dose of skepticism (and maybe a pinch of sarcasm).

The Hype Cycle: From Inflated Expectations to the Trough of Disillusionment (and Back Again)

Like any emerging technology, AI is subject to the hype cycle. First, we have the peak of inflated expectations, where everyone is convinced that AI will solve all our problems and usher in a utopia of unprecedented productivity and prosperity. But then, reality sets in, and we tumble into the trough of disillusionment, realizing that AI isn't a magic bullet and that it comes with its own set of limitations and challenges.

But don't despair! The hype cycle doesn't end there. As we learn more about AI's capabilities and limitations, we begin to climb the slope of enlightenment, where we develop a more nuanced understanding of what AI can and cannot do. And eventually, we reach the plateau of productivity, where AI becomes an integral part of our lives, enhancing our work, our creativity, and our overall well-being.

The Reality Check: AI is a Tool, Not a Miracle Worker

Let's be clear: AI is a tool, not a miracle worker. It can't solve all our problems, and it won't magically transform our lives overnight. But it *can* help us work smarter, not harder. It can automate tedious tasks, generate creative ideas, and provide insights that we might not have discovered on our own.

Think of it like a trusty hammer: it won't build a house for you, but it can sure make the process a whole lot easier.

The Dangers of Hype: Unrealistic Expectations and Disappointment

The problem with hype is that it sets us up for disappointment. When we expect AI to be a magical solution to all our problems, we're bound to be disappointed when it falls short. This can lead to disillusionment, skepticism, and even backlash against AI technology.

That's why it's so important to have a balanced perspective. We need to embrace AI's potential while also acknowledging its limitations. We need to set realistic expectations and understand that AI is a tool that we can use to achieve our goals, not a panacea that will solve all our problems.

The Romero Perspective: A Call for Pragmatism (and a Dash of Humor)

So, how do we navigate the hype surrounding AI? Here's my advice:

- **Be Realistic:** Don't believe the hype. AI is not a magic bullet, and it won't solve all our problems overnight.
- **Be Curious:** Learn about AI and its capabilities, but don't be afraid to ask questions and challenge assumptions.
- **Be Open-Minded:** Embrace the possibilities of AI, but also be aware of its limitations and potential risks.
- **Be Patient:** AI is still a young technology, and it's constantly evolving. Don't expect it to be perfect, but be open to the possibilities it holds.

And most importantly, don't take it too seriously! AI might be changing the world, but it doesn't have to be all doom and gloom. Let's have some fun with it, explore its creative potential, and use it to make our lives a little bit easier and a whole lot more interesting.

Ethical Frameworks:

AI's Rulebook (Think "Thou Shalt Not Create Skynet," But Less Dramatic)

Alright, AI enthusiasts and ethical explorers, let's talk about rules. No, not the boring kind your parents made you follow when you were a kid (though those were probably important too). We're talking about ethical frameworks for AI – the guidelines and principles that keep our artificially intelligent pals from turning into power-hungry supervillains.

Why Rules Matter, Even for Robots (Especially for Robots)

Think of it this way: even the most well-intentioned kid needs some boundaries, right? Without rules, they might accidentally set the house on fire while trying to make s'mores. Similarly, AI needs some guardrails to ensure it's used for good, not evil.

Ethical frameworks provide those guardrails, guiding the development and use of AI in a way that's safe, fair, and beneficial to society. They help us answer tough questions like:

- Should AI systems be allowed to make life-or-death decisions?
- How can we prevent AI from perpetuating harmful biases and discrimination?

- Who is responsible when AI goes wrong?
- Should we prioritize human well-being over AI efficiency?

Building a Better AI: The Ethical Framework Toolkit

Thankfully, there's no shortage of ethical frameworks for AI. These guidelines offer a set of principles and best practices that can help us navigate the complex ethical landscape of AI development and use.

Some of the most prominent frameworks include:

- **The Asilomar AI Principles:** A set of 23 principles developed by AI researchers and thought leaders, covering topics like safety, transparency, and human values.
- **The OECD Principles on AI:** A set of five principles adopted by the Organisation for Economic Co-operation and Development (OECD) to promote the responsible stewardship of trustworthy AI.
- **The European Union's Ethics Guidelines for Trustworthy AI:** A comprehensive framework for developing and deploying AI systems that are lawful, ethical, and robust.

Real-World Examples: AI Ethics in Action

Ethical AI isn't just a theoretical concept; it's being put into practice by organizations around the world.

- **Google:** Has developed its own set of AI Principles that guide its research and development efforts.
- **Microsoft:** Has established the Aether Committee to oversee its AI ethics and ensure responsible AI practices.
- **OpenAI:** Is actively researching ways to make AI more transparent, explainable, and aligned with human values.

The Ethical AI Challenge: It's a Marathon, Not a Sprint

Developing ethical AI is an ongoing challenge, not a one-and-done deal. As AI technology continues to evolve, so too must our ethical frameworks. We need to constantly reassess our assumptions, adapt to new challenges, and engage in open and honest dialogue about the implications of AI for our society.

The Romero Perspective: A Call to Action

AI has the potential to be an incredible force for good, but only if we use it wisely and ethically. That's why it's so important for everyone – from developers and policymakers to businesses and consumers – to take an active role in shaping the ethical landscape of AI.

So, let's roll up our sleeves, get involved in the conversation, and work together to build a future where AI serves humanity, not the other way around. It's a big challenge, but hey, we humans are pretty good at tackling big challenges, aren't we?

CHAPTER SEVENTEEN

My AI Odyssey:

From Skeptic to Copilot Convert (Confessions of a Tech Cynic)

Alright, folks, let's get personal. We've spent this entire book geeking out over Copilot's features, dissecting its inner workings, and pondering its ethical implications. But now it's time for a confession: I wasn't always a Copilot believer. In fact, I was downright skeptical when I first heard about it.

The Skeptic's Lament: "Another AI Assistant? Really?"

Like many of you, I've seen my fair share of AI assistants come and go. From Clippy's cringeworthy attempts at humor to Siri's often-clueless responses, I'd grown weary of the promises of AI-powered productivity. So, when Copilot burst onto the scene, I rolled my eyes and muttered, "Another AI assistant? Really?"

I envisioned a glorified autocomplete tool that would spit out generic suggestions and barely scratch the surface of what I needed. But boy, was I wrong.

The Copilot Conversion: A Journey of Discovery and Delight

My skepticism quickly melted away as I started experimenting with Copilot. It wasn't just a glorified autocomplete tool; it was a creative collaborator, a brainstorming buddy, and even a debugging guru.

I was amazed by its ability to understand my writing style, anticipate my needs, and offer suggestions that were both helpful and surprising. It was like having a virtual writing partner who could tap into my subconscious and pull out ideas that I didn't even know I had.

But Copilot wasn't just a writer's tool. It also helped me tackle complex spreadsheets, analyze data, and even generate code snippets. It was like having a team of experts at my fingertips, always ready to lend a hand (or a brain).

The Aha! Moment:

When Copilot Became Indispensable

The real turning point for me came when I was working on a particularly challenging project. I was stuck, frustrated, and ready to give up. But then, I turned to Copilot for help. With a few simple prompts, it was able to generate a solution that I'd never have thought of on my own. It was a true "aha!" moment, and it solidified Copilot's place in my workflow.

From that moment on, Copilot became an indispensable part of my work life. It helped me write faster, think clearer, and even have more fun. It became my trusted sidekick, my creative muse, and my go-to resource for all things digital.

The Romero Verdict: Copilot is a Game-Changer (and a Friend)

My journey with Copilot has been a revelation. It's shown me that AI isn't just a buzzword or a futuristic fantasy; it's a practical tool that can truly enhance our lives. But more than that, it's shown me that AI can be fun, creative, and even a little bit magical.

So, if you're still on the fence about Copilot, I urge you to give it a try. You might just be surprised at how much you like it. And who knows, you might even find yourself wondering how you ever lived without it.

The Wonders of AI:

Welcome to the Future, Where Your Brain Gets a Bionic Boost (No Assembly Required!)

Buckle up, fellow humans, because we're about to embark on a mind-blowing tour of AI's potential to transform our lives. Forget those dystopian visions of robot overlords and sentient toasters (though, who wouldn't want a toaster that makes the *perfect* bagel?). We're talking about the real, tangible ways that AI is already making our lives easier, healthier, and more fulfilling.

More Than Just a Fancy Calculator: AI's Superpowers Unveiled

AI isn't just about number crunching and data analysis (though it's pretty darn good at that too). It's about amplifying human potential, pushing the boundaries of what's possible, and creating a future that's smarter, more efficient, and dare we say, even a little bit magical.

Imagine a world where:

- **Doctors** have AI-powered sidekicks that can diagnose diseases with superhuman accuracy, allowing for earlier intervention and better outcomes.
- **Scientists** use AI to accelerate research, discover new drugs, and even model complex systems like climate change.
- **Artists** collaborate with AI to create new forms of music, art, and literature that challenge our perceptions and expand our imaginations.
- **Engineers** design smarter cities, more efficient transportation systems, and buildings that can adapt to our needs.

- **Everyday People** use AI to automate mundane tasks, freeing up time for creativity, connection, and personal growth.

This isn't science fiction, folks. It's happening right now. AI is already transforming industries, empowering individuals, and changing the world as we know it.

Real-World Wonders: AI's Impact on Everyday Life

Here are just a few examples of how AI is already making a difference in our lives:

- **Healthcare:** AI-powered tools are helping doctors detect cancer earlier, predict patient outcomes, and personalize treatment plans.
- **Education:** AI is being used to create personalized learning experiences, identify struggling students, and provide targeted support.
- **Agriculture:** AI-powered drones and sensors are helping farmers optimize crop yields, reduce waste, and minimize their environmental impact.
- **Transportation:** Self-driving cars and trucks are poised to revolutionize the way we travel, making roads safer and reducing traffic congestion.

- **Accessibility:** AI-powered assistive technologies are helping people with disabilities live more independent and fulfilling lives.

The AI-Powered Future: A World of Possibilities (and a Few Challenges)

The potential of AI is truly mind-boggling. It has the power to transform our world in ways we can only imagine. But with great power comes great responsibility.

We need to ensure that AI is developed and used ethically, responsibly, and for the benefit of all. We need to address concerns about bias, job displacement, and the potential for misuse of this powerful technology.

But if we can rise to the challenge, the future of AI is incredibly bright. It's a future where we can work smarter, live healthier, and connect with each other in more meaningful ways.

The Romero Perspective: A Call to Embrace the AI Adventure

AI is an incredible journey that's just beginning. It's a journey filled with both challenges and opportunities, with the potential to transform our world in unimaginable ways.

So, let's embrace this AI adventure with a sense of wonder and excitement. Let's explore its possibilities, learn from its mistakes, and work together to create a future where AI serves humanity, not the other way around.

A Call to Action: Don't Be a Dinosaur, Embrace Your Inner AI Jedi (No Lightsaber Required, But Seriously, Get on Board!)

Alright, fellow humans, it's time to stop dragging your feet and join the AI revolution! We've explored the wonders, the quirks, and the ethical dilemmas of AI. Now it's time to take action.

Embrace the Future, One Click (or Voice Command) at a Time

The future of work is here, and it's powered by AI. Whether you're a writer, a coder, a marketer, or a data analyst, AI tools like Copilot can supercharge your productivity, unleash your creativity, and open up a world of new possibilities.

But here's the thing: AI isn't just about technology; it's about mindset. It's about embracing change, being open to new ideas, and having the courage to experiment. It's about seeing AI not as a threat, but as a partner, a collaborator, a co-pilot on your journey to success.

Your Mission, Should You Choose to Accept It (And You Should):

- **Explore:** Dive into the world of AI tools. Try out Copilot, experiment with different prompts and features, and see how it can enhance your work.

- **Learn:** Don't be afraid to ask questions, seek guidance, and learn from others. The AI community is vibrant and supportive, with countless resources and tutorials available.
- **Share:** Tell your friends, colleagues, and family about the amazing things you're doing with AI. Spread the word and help others embrace this transformative technology.
- **Advocate:** Be a voice for responsible AI development and use. Demand transparency, fairness, and accountability from AI creators and companies.
- **Create:** Use AI to unleash your creativity and build amazing things. Write that novel, code that app, launch that business. The possibilities are endless!

The AI Advantage: It's Not Just About Productivity, It's About Potential

AI isn't just about making our lives easier (though that's a pretty sweet perk). It's about unlocking our full potential as humans. It's about giving us the tools and resources we need to solve problems, create art, and make a positive impact on the world.

So, don't be a dinosaur, clinging to outdated ways of working. Embrace your inner AI Jedi, harness the power of technology, and let's build a future that's smarter, more creative, and more equitable for all. The force is strong with this one (and by "this one," I mean AI, of course).

Remember: The future is what we make of it. Let's choose to make it a future where humans and AI work together in harmony, where technology serves us, not the other way around. So, what are you waiting for? The AI revolution is calling!

Key Takeaways:

Copilot's Greatest Hits (A Cheat Sheet for Your Brain)

Alright, fellow Copilot aficionados, let's take a victory lap and recap the highlights of our AI-powered adventure. We've covered a lot of ground, from mastering prompts to unleashing Copilot's creative genius to pondering the ethical implications of AI. But before we bid adieu (for now), let's distill all that knowledge into a few key takeaways that you can tuck away in your mental toolbox.

Copilot's Key Features: The Swiss Army Knife of AI Assistants

Copilot isn't just a one-trick pony; it's a multi-talented powerhouse with a wide range of capabilities. Here are a few of its greatest hits:

- **Writing Wizard:** From emails to essays to code, Copilot can help you write faster, smarter, and more creatively.
- **Data Dynamo:** Analyze data, build spreadsheets, and generate insights like a pro, even if you're not a math whiz.
- **Presentation Pro:** Create stunning slide decks that captivate your audience and leave a lasting impression.
- **Coding Companion:** Write cleaner code, debug faster, and even explore new programming languages with ease.
- **Automation Ace:** Automate repetitive tasks, streamline workflows, and reclaim your time for more meaningful work.
- **Creative Collaborator:** Brainstorm ideas, craft fiction, and generate marketing copy that sizzles.
- **Language Learner:** Translate text, understand code logic, and even learn new languages.
- **And so much more!**

The Copilot Benefit Bonanza: More Than Just Productivity

Copilot isn't just about getting things done faster; it's about working smarter, unlocking your creativity, and even having a little fun along the way. Here are just a few of the benefits you can reap from using Copilot:

- **Increased Productivity:** Automate tasks, streamline workflows, and get more done in less time.
- **Enhanced Creativity:** Brainstorm ideas, explore new possibilities, and push the boundaries of your imagination.
- **Improved Learning:** Learn new skills, expand your knowledge, and stay ahead of the curve.
- **Reduced Stress:** Let Copilot handle the mundane tasks so you can focus on the work that matters.
- **More Fun at Work:** Inject some personality and humor into your work with Copilot's witty suggestions and playful interactions.

The Copilot Effect: A Ripple of Change

Copilot isn't just changing the way individuals work; it's also transforming industries, redefining job roles, and shaping the future of work itself. It's a powerful tool that has the potential to democratize access to information, empower creativity, and create a more inclusive and equitable workplace.

The Romero Prognosis: The Future is Bright (and AI-Powered)

The future of work is here, and it's AI-powered. Copilot is just the beginning of a wave of intelligent tools that will change the way we work and live. So, embrace the change, harness the power of AI, and get ready to soar to new heights of productivity and creativity.

Remember: Copilot is more than just an AI assistant; it's a partner, a collaborator, and a catalyst for change. With Copilot by your side, the possibilities are endless.

Advice for Getting Started:

From Copilot Rookie to AI Ace (No Training Montage Required!)

Alright, my fellow productivity Padawans, it's time to put all that Copilot knowledge into action! We've explored the features, the benefits, and even the quirks of this AI sidekick. Now, let's roll up our sleeves and get down to business with some practical tips for maximizing Copilot's value in your everyday work.

Copilot Bootcamp: Your Training Plan for AI Mastery

Think of this as your Copilot bootcamp, a crash course in becoming an AI-powered productivity ninja. We'll cover everything from mastering prompts to taming your inbox to conquering writer's block. So, grab your metaphorical sweatband and let's get started!

1. **Start with the Basics:** Don't try to tackle everything at once. Begin by experimenting with Copilot's core features, such as text generation, summarization, and translation. Get a feel for how it works and how it can fit into your workflow.

2. **Master the Art of the Prompt:** Remember, Copilot is only as good as the instructions you give it. Take some time to learn the art of prompt engineering. Be specific, provide context, and don't be afraid to experiment with different phrasing.

3. **Embrace the Feedback Loop:** Copilot is always learning and improving. Your feedback is crucial to its growth. So, don't be shy about giving it a thumbs up or thumbs down, and provide specific suggestions for improvement.

4. **Explore the Integrations:** Copilot isn't just a standalone tool; it integrates with a wide range of other

apps and platforms. Explore these integrations and see how you can leverage Copilot's power in your favorite tools.

5. **Think Outside the Box:** Don't limit yourself to the obvious use cases. Get creative and see how you can use Copilot to tackle new challenges and solve problems in unexpected ways.

Real-World Tips from Copilot Pros:

- **Set Goals:** Before you start using Copilot, take some time to define your goals. What do you want to achieve? What challenges are you facing? How can Copilot help you overcome them?

- **Experiment:** Don't be afraid to try new things and push Copilot's limits. You might be surprised at what it can do.

- **Be Patient:** Copilot is still learning and evolving. Don't get discouraged if it doesn't always get it right. With time and practice, it will become an indispensable tool in your arsenal.

- **Have Fun:** Don't forget to have fun with Copilot! It's a powerful tool, but it's also a creative partner and a source of inspiration. Enjoy the journey!

Your AI-Powered Adventure Awaits:

With these tips in hand, you're ready to embark on your own AI-powered adventure. So, go forth and conquer! The future of work is yours to shape, and Copilot is here to help you every step of the way.

The Road Ahead:

Buckle Up, Buttercup! The AI Adventure is Just Beginning (and It's Gonna Be a Wild Ride)

Alright, fellow AI explorers, as we reach the end of our journey through the world of Copilot, it's time to take a moment and gaze into the crystal ball of the future. (Don't worry, no hocus-pocus here, just some good old-fashioned speculation based on the current trajectory of AI innovation.)

Beyond Copilot: The AI Evolution is Unstoppable

[Image: A vibrant, futuristic cityscape with AI-powered vehicles, robots, and holographic displays]

Let's be honest: we've barely scratched the surface of what AI can do. Copilot is an impressive tool, but it's just a glimpse of what's to come. In the coming years, we can expect AI to become even more integrated into our lives, transforming how we work, learn, create, and even play.

Imagine a world where:

- **AI-Powered Personal Assistants:** These digital sidekicks will anticipate our needs, schedule our appointments, and even help us manage our emotions.
- **Hyper-Personalized Education:** AI tutors will adapt to each student's individual learning style and pace, providing tailored instruction and feedback.
- **Creative Collaborators:** AI will co-create art, music, and literature with humans, pushing the boundaries of creativity and imagination.
- **Medical Marvels:** AI will diagnose diseases earlier, develop personalized treatments, and even perform complex surgeries with superhuman precision.
- **Environmental Guardians:** AI will help us monitor and protect our planet, from predicting natural disasters to optimizing energy consumption to developing sustainable solutions.

Challenges and Opportunities: A Bumpy Ride, but Worth It

Of course, the road to the AI-powered future won't be without its bumps and detours. We'll face challenges like job displacement, ethical dilemmas, and the potential for misuse of this powerful technology.

But with every challenge comes an opportunity. By embracing AI with a spirit of curiosity, collaboration, and ethical responsibility, we can harness its power to create a better world for ourselves and future generations.

The Romero Prognosis: The Future is Bright (and Full of Surprises)

I'm not a fortune teller (although I do have a pretty cool collection of tarot cards), but I'm optimistic about the future of AI. I believe it has the potential to revolutionize our lives in ways we can't even imagine.

So, let's embrace this AI adventure with open minds and open hearts. Let's explore, experiment, and push the boundaries of what's possible. And most importantly, let's have some fun along the way!

Remember: The future is not something that happens to us; it's something we create. So, let's roll up our sleeves, grab our digital tools, and get to work building the AI-powered world of our dreams.

I hope this Romero-style conclusion provides the perfect ending to your comprehensive guide to Copilot. Let me know if you need any further refinements or adjustments!

CONCLUSION

The Future is Copilot-ed! (Or: How I Learned to Stop Worrying and Love the AI)

Well, dear readers, we've reached the end of our whirlwind tour through the wild world of Copilot. We've laughed, we've learned, we've maybe even shed a tear or two (mostly from frustration with finicky formulas). But through it all, one thing is clear: Copilot is a game-changer. It's the AI sidekick we didn't know we needed, the digital assistant that's always got our back, the creative muse that never runs out of ideas.

Your Copilot Adventure: A Recap

We've covered a lot of ground in this book, from the basics of installation and setup to the intricacies of prompt engineering, from the nitty-gritty of troubleshooting to the ethical implications of AI.

We've seen how Copilot can:

- **Transform your inbox** from a chaotic mess into a Zen garden of productivity.
- **Elevate your writing** from "meh" to magnificent.
- **Supercharge your coding** with intelligent suggestions and automated refactoring.

- **Unleash your inner data wizard**, revealing hidden insights and transforming numbers into captivating stories.
- **Transform your presentations** from snooze-fests to standing ovations.
- **And so much more!**

The Road Ahead: A Future Filled with AI-Powered Possibilities

But this is just the beginning. As AI continues to evolve, we can expect Copilot (and other AI assistants) to become even more powerful, intuitive, and integrated into our lives. Imagine a future where:

- **Creativity is unleashed:** AI-powered tools help us generate groundbreaking ideas and express ourselves in new and exciting ways.
- **Collaboration is seamless:** Humans and AI work together seamlessly, leveraging their respective strengths to achieve incredible results.
- **Work becomes more meaningful:** Tedious tasks are automated, freeing us to focus on work that's challenging, fulfilling, and impactful.

A Word of Caution (Because Romero Always Keeps it Real):

The AI revolution is not without its challenges. We need to be mindful of the potential for bias, job displacement, and misuse of this powerful technology. But by approaching AI with a critical eye, a collaborative spirit, and a commitment to ethical principles, we can create a future where AI benefits us all.

The Romero Prognosis: The Future is Bright (and AI-Powered!)

I'm not a fortune teller (although I do make a mean margarita), but I'm optimistic about the future of AI. I believe it has the potential to transform our lives for the better, if we use it wisely and responsibly.

So, my fellow adventurers, let's embrace this AI-powered future with open arms (and maybe a healthy dose of skepticism). Let's continue to learn, explore, and experiment with Copilot and other AI tools. And let's work together to build a world where AI is a force for good, not evil.

The future is ours to create, and with Copilot by our side, who knows what amazing things we can achieve?

APPENDIX

Your Copilot Survival Kit

Alright, fellow Copilot adventurers, we've reached the end of our journey (for now, at least). You've become a prompt-whispering, code-crunching, data-visualizing, presentation-mastering AI ninja. But before we bid you adieu, we wanted to equip you with a few extra goodies to ensure your continued success in the ever-evolving world of AI.

Troubleshooting Toolbox:

- **Copilot's Not Responding!** Don't panic. First, try restarting your computer. If that doesn't work, check your internet connection. Still no luck? Reach out to the Copilot community or Microsoft support for help.
- **Copilot's Gone Rogue!** If Copilot starts spouting nonsense or acting strangely, try resetting its settings to default. If that doesn't work, it might be time for a full uninstall and reinstall.
- **I Need More Power!** If you're looking for even more advanced troubleshooting tips or want to dive into the nitty-gritty of Copilot's inner workings, check out the official Microsoft documentation or explore online forums and communities.

Resource Roundup:

- **Official Copilot Website:** Your one-stop shop for all things Copilot.
- **Microsoft Learn:** Find tutorials, courses, and certifications to level up your Copilot skills.
- **Copilot Community Forums:** Connect with fellow Copilot users, ask questions, and share your knowledge.
- **AI Ethics Resources:** Learn more about the ethical implications of AI and how to use it responsibly. (We recommend starting with Chapter 13!)

The Romero Prognostication: What's Next for Copilot?

While we can't predict the future with absolute certainty (we're writers, not fortune tellers), we can say with confidence that Copilot is just getting started. We can expect to see even more impressive features, deeper integrations, and even more mind-blowing capabilities in the years to come.

So, stay curious, keep learning, and never stop exploring the possibilities of AI. The future is bright, and it's Copilot-ed!

INDEX

- Design Dynamo: Create Stunning Slides (Even If You're Design-Challenged)
- Content Creator: From Blank Slides to Brilliant Ideas
- Rehearsal Room: Practice Makes Perfect (or at Least, Less Awkward)
- Audience Engager: Turning Spectators into Superfans

Section III: Copilot Pro Tips: Taking Your Skills to 11

Chapter 9: Customization Overlord: Mold Your AI Sidekick to Perfection

- Voice & Tone: From Shakespearean Scholar to Stand-Up Comic
- Domain Expertise: Teaching Copilot Your Industry Secrets
- Under the Hood: Advanced Settings for Power Users

Chapter 10: Troubleshooting 911: When Copilot Needs a Time-Out

- Copilot Conundrum: Common Causes of AI Angst
- Troubleshooting Toolkit: Your Copilot Rescue Mission
- Copilot Zen: Embrace the Quirks (and Laugh It Off)

- Troubleshooting Toolbox: When Copilot Needs a Time-Out
- Resource Roundup: Websites, Forums, and More
- Romero's Parting Words: A Few Final Thoughts (and Maybe a Dad Joke)

Additional Resources

Hey there, fellow Copilot enthusiast!

I'm thrilled you embarked on this AI-powered journey with me through the pages of Microsoft Copilot Users Guide. If you found yourself chuckling, nodding along, and maybe even having a few "aha!" moments, then my mission is accomplished!

But now, it's your turn to spread the Copilot love! Here's how you can help:

- **Tell your friends:** Know someone who's still struggling with email overload, writer's block, or code conundrums? Share this book with them and watch their productivity soar (and their stress levels plummet).
- **Leave a review:** Your honest feedback is invaluable! Head over to Amazon or your favourite online bookseller and let the world know what you think of *Microsoft Copilot Users Guide*. Your review can help other readers discover this gem of a guide and embark on their own Copilot adventures.
- **Share on social media:** Spread the AI love on your favourite social media platforms.

Remember, the AI revolution is here, and Copilot is leading the charge. By sharing your positive experience with others, you're not just helping them become more productive; you're also shaping the future of work and creativity.

Thanks again for joining me on this AI-powered journey!

Cheers,

Patrick K. Romero.

P.S. If you have any questions or need further Copilot guidance, don't hesitate to reach out. I'm always here to help! Drop by my Author Central page and let's connect!